THE PURSUIT
OF PURPOSE

To Michael

THE PURSUIT OF PURPOSE

DISCOVERING TRUE FULFILLMENT IN OUR SEARCH FOR MORE

TYLER WEDELL

NEW DEGREE PRESS

THE PURSUIT OF PURPOSE
Discovering True Fulfillment in Our Search for More

ISBN 978-1-63730-455-6 *Paperback*
     978-1-63730-567-6 *Kindle Ebook*
     978-1-63730-568-3 *Ebook*

To my Heavenly Father,
for creating me with purpose.
Your will be done.

CONTENTS

"*The purpose of life is not to be happy.
It is to be useful, to be honorable, to be
compassionate, to have it make some difference
that you have lived and lived well.*"

—RALPH WALDO EMERSON

INTRODUCTION

———

The pursuit of happiness has become an expected human right ingrained in the fabric of America. The opportunity to attain a life full of the material things, people, and achievements that bring us happiness is the American Dream. Many view this as the primary aim in life. Yet why is it that when we look at those who appear to have reached this goal, happiness is the farthest thing from their experience?

Take, for example, Michael Phelps. He is the most decorated Olympian of all time, winning a staggering twenty-eight medals in his Olympic career. His success in the swimming pool propelled him into several large endorsement deals, setting him up financially for life. By the time he was nineteen years old, he had everything—wealth, fame, success, connections—all on a global platform. He could literally do or have anything he wanted. Yet despite these tremendous accomplishments, he struggled with recurring episodes of depression that landed him in rehab.[1]

So many people look at the success of Michael Phelps and assume that because he had everything, he should be happy. Yet he wasn't. He was miserable. It wasn't until he hit rock bottom that he was forced to look at life differently. Only then did he discover a path to true fulfillment. His journey of accomplishing everything he wanted, yet not finding happiness, was not a unique story. It turns out there is a broader trend of this, along with the devastating mental health side effects present in other people's lives.

According to the CDC, from 1999 through to 2018, the number of suicides per year increased by 35 percent. Suicide is now the second leading cause of death for people aged ten to thirty-four.[2] Loneliness, depression, and anxiety are also on the rise. According to a 2020 survey by Cigna, 61 percent of Americans said they were lonely, up 7 percentage points from two years ago. Major depressive episodes increased by 19 percent between 2005 and 2014 for those aged twelve to twenty-five.[3] And the onset of the COVID-19 pandemic has only made things even worse.

The United States was founded as the land of opportunity where one is free to pursue the American Dream. Our founding fathers etched this into our Declaration of Independence to preserve for us the inalienable rights of life, liberty, and the pursuit of happiness. That has become the primary influence in our culture as we strive to attain all that makes us happy. But as the statistics show, it isn't working.

At the same time, we are becoming less faith-oriented. Over the past decade, the number of people in the United States who are religiously unaffiliated has grown by 74 percent.[4] Additionally, the number of Christians has decreased by 6 percent.[5] In other words, people are leaving their faith, and many are choosing not to identify with any religion at all. These trends show a nation of people who have taken fate into their own hands as they pursue happiness relentlessly and with a one-dimensional perspective.

Could it be that our attempts to acquire all that we think will satisfy and make us happy are misguided? The countless people that we idolize for possessing everything we could ever want are still searching for more. It's not that happiness is a bad thing to have or even desire, but when we make it the key thing we are living for, we set ourselves up for failure. Our focus turns to things outside of ourselves to fulfill us, building our lives on an unstable foundation driven by social media, culture, and our own desires. It is impossible to keep up with our appetite for more, leaving us never truly fulfilled. But I believe there is a better path, one that I discovered the hard way and now hope to illuminate for others to find more easily.

When I was in high school, I focused on living solely for the weekends as I sought every opportunity to have as much fun as possible. I got good grades, excelled on the golf team, and mostly stayed out of trouble. But even though I appeared to be a normal high school kid, I wrestled with difficult emotions and bouts of depression. In one of my lowest moments, I questioned why I was even alive; what was the point of my life? Left with no answers, I became apathetic and clung to more of what I thought would make me happy—drinking and partying with my friends every chance I got.

But it only added to the volatility of my emotions and left me feeling stuck. One year, during this challenging time in high school, I received a book about finding your purpose while attending a Christmas Eve service at church. My family and I only went to services for the major holidays each year, and this was the first time they ever handed out a free book. I was in a lot of emotional pain, and its premise intrigued me; so, I started reading it.

For the first time in my life, it opened my eyes to the reality that God had created me for a reason, for a purpose bigger than myself. This revelation was exhilarating. It gave me a sense of hope for my future and planted in me a seed that would eventually grow to change my life forever. Coincidentally, I later found out I had something in common with Michael Phelps—we both read the same book that launched us on a journey to discover our purpose.

I wish I could say it was all smooth sailing from there, but it wasn't. I bounced between this new hope I had and my old focus on living solely for myself. It wasn't until after graduating high school that my life reflected this truth— that living a life of significance and meaning is profoundly more satisfying than selfishly pursuing happiness. But what I discovered isn't just true for me; it's true for you too. Your life has a meaning that is bigger than the endless pursuit of chasing what makes you happy. Living for a greater purpose leads to a substantially more fulfilling life, which begs the question: how do we find such purpose? That is the journey I'd like to invite you on.

After discovering that my life had meaning, I became passionate about sharing what I learned with others. This book is the culmination of my desire to help people discover their purpose. In the pages that follow, we will explore the areas in our lives we can look at to find meaning. Armed with this knowledge, we can stop chasing temporary happiness and begin finding purpose in our everyday lives. If you can relate to the feeling of emptiness or void in your life that something seems to be missing—then this book is for you. Or maybe you have a desire to do something great with your life but aren't sure where to start. Whatever led you to be curious about your purpose, this book will give you the tools to find it.

Over the coming chapters, you will hear more of my story and the stories of others who have encountered meaning in their lives. You will learn about the journeys they went through and what it took for them to find a purpose that gave them something greater to live for each day. We will unpack the attributes these people possess and the places within their lives they looked to discover their calling. I hope the pages that follow will encourage, equip, and inspire you to pursue purpose in your own life and lead you to experience a deep sense of joy that is more fulfilling than the pursuit of fleeting happiness.

PART I

THE FOUNDATION

PART 1

THE FOUNDATION

1

THE PURSUIT

—

"True happiness is not attained through self-gratification, but through fidelity to a worthy purpose."

—HELEN KELLER

Michael Phelps competed in his first Olympic games in 2000, at fifteen years old. He became the youngest American male swimmer to enter the Olympic Games in sixty-eight years. By the time he was nineteen, he had set five world records and had won seven Olympic medals in Athens, almost breaking the record for most gold medals won at the Olympics. Multi-million-dollar sponsorship deals followed his achievements as companies pursued him to sign with their brand.

When he retired from the Olympics in 2012, he had become the most decorated Olympian in history. "I accomplished every goal I ever wanted to ... I've done everything I ever wanted to do ... and, at that point, it's just time to move on," Michael said, solidifying his intention to end his career.

Asked what he would do next, Phelps responded, "After the summer, I really don't know what I'm going to do."[6]

But despite all his success, there was a recurring pattern happening behind the scenes. After every Olympics he competed in, Phelps fell into depression and turned to drinking to find happiness. He got his first DUI in the same year he won his first five gold medals. He apologized publicly for his behavior and vowed to do better going forward. But it was clear his struggle to be happy was becoming increasingly more challenging as his success grew. The thrill of breaking more records and winning more medals was losing its appeal. In a 2016 interview with the *New York Times*, Phelps described it this way: "It's like we dreamed the biggest dream we could possibly dream, and we got there. What do we do now?" As the reality of what might follow set in and the excitement of the games wore off, Michael fell back into an emotional lull as his battle with depression returned.

He coasted into the 2012 Olympics in London, being the least prepared he had ever been, but still added six medals to his career to become the most decorated Olympian in history. After that performance, he announced his retirement. Having worked so hard to accomplish all that he had in his swimming career, he was ready to enjoy his life and travel the world. He embarked on this new chapter with the aim of just relaxing and maximizing the enjoyment of his time, but he continued to struggle with being happy. Two years after he retired, Phelps was pulled over and arrested again for a DUI—his second offense in ten years.

That was the moment Phelps had hit rock bottom. He didn't leave his bedroom for five days straight—didn't sleep, didn't eat, just curled up in a ball. He ridiculed himself over how many times he could mess up. "I was a train wreck. Like a time bomb waiting to go off ... I had no self-esteem, no self-worth," Phelps recalled in a 2016 interview with ESPN. "For a moment, I thought it was going to be the end of my life."

During the week following Phelps's second DUI, his close friends and family reached out to him, concerned for his mental health. One of his friends, Ray Lewis, called and encouraged him not to give up as he shared with him some of his own personal struggles. Phelps decided to go to a rehab center for forty-five days. For the first time in his life, he did some deep introspective work. He began seeing a counselor and reading several books. One book, in particular, had a profound impact on him: *The Purpose Driven Life* by Rick Warren. After finishing it, Phelps was overwhelmed with newfound hope and energy at what he had discovered: "It's turned me into believing there is a power greater than myself and there is a purpose for me on this planet."[7]

Phelps emerged from rehab as a new man. His time there equipped him with a different outlook on life and a profound fresh awareness that he had a bigger purpose than swimming and winning Olympic medals. Not sure what that purpose looked like yet, Phelps came out of retirement and competed in one more Olympics to end his career on better terms. He talked publicly about his battle with mental health and realized that his challenges with depression and anxiety weren't just something he struggled with; it was prevalent among other Olympic athletes.

At that moment, it hit him. Maybe his purpose in life was to call attention to the mental health struggles within the Olympic community—to let other athletes know they are not alone and encourage them to get help. The thought of that gave Phelps a lot of energy. He embraced this new mission and co-produced the HBO documentary *The*

Weight of Gold, where Phelps and other prominent Olympic athletes shared their struggles with depression, anxiety, and suicide. By opening up this dialog on mental health, Phelps helped others find strength in knowing that it's okay to not be okay. Living out this new purpose changed his outlook on life and proved to be more satisfying than anything else he had achieved in his career. "For me, that's way bigger than ever winning gold medals," Phelps said. "The chance to potentially save a life, to give that person an opportunity to grow and learn and help someone else, there's nothing better in life."[8]

Phelps had everything he could ask for, yet happiness eluded him. He was popular, had tremendous wealth, and was retired, leaving him the freedom to do whatever he pleased. But those ingredients didn't lead him to contentment. He ended up instead feeling restless and depressed as he searched for what was missing in his life. His struggle to find happiness should prompt us to look at our own journey. Are we focused on trying to discover what is missing in our lives as well? Do we think that the answer to becoming happy will be found once we have the means to do and acquire whatever we please?

Our ability to learn from the experiences of others will help us avoid a considerable amount of pain and heartache. Phelps's journey to happiness seemed like a simple matter of filling his life with all the things he enjoyed doing. There was nothing standing in his way once he retired. But we can learn from him and others who have the world at their fingertips. The struggle so many successful people face with finding true fulfillment in life should be a wake-up call for us all. If the search for happiness through money, fame, and excess has not produced a deeply fulfilling life, then maybe we are chasing after the wrong thing. Instead of making our priority to fill our lives with that which will bring us the greatest enjoyment, let's consider what Phelps explored and ask ourselves if we have a deeper purpose to live for. If the discovery of meaning and significance was powerful enough to turn Phelps's life around, perhaps our pursuits should also focus on finding purpose instead of chasing happiness.

THE PURSUIT OF HAPPINESS

The pursuit of happiness is defined as the drive to attain that which will produce a pleasurable or satisfying experience. This definition leaves much to be interpreted by the one seeking to be happy, but when someone is in a position where they possess the means to get or do anything they want, shouldn't happiness follow? If we eliminated the time and money barriers in our life, it would seem natural that attaining happiness would come next, but that doesn't guarantee that it will. Not only did happiness fail to materialize for Phelps, but there are other examples of people who also seemed to have everything yet were still searching for something more.

Tom Brady, an icon in the football world, holds the title for the most Super Bowl wins of any player or coach in the NFL. Halfway into his career, he felt a similar longing to the one Phelps had. "Why do I have three Super Bowl rings and still think there's something greater out there for me?" Brady said. "I mean, maybe a lot of people would say, 'Hey man, this is what is.' I reached my goal, my dream, my life. Me, I think: God, it's gotta be more than this. I mean, this can't be what it's all cracked up to be. I mean, I've done it. I'm twenty-seven. And what else is there for me?"[9]

Josh Radnor, famously known for playing Ted Mosby in the show *How I Met Your Mother*, described what it was like after the show's success led to his fame and opened up a world of endless opportunities. "A lot of people try to lure you: 'Come here, drink this, look at her, she'll talk to you.' There's all sorts of temptations that offer themselves," he says. "For the first year or two of *How I Met Your Mother*, I was like, *'Well, I guess this is what guys in my position do.'* And it left me feeling really empty, and more than a little depressed."[10]

Brian Welch—lead guitarist and founding member of the heavy metal band Korn—is another example. In the mid-nineties, his band created a new subgenre of metal music and became wildly popular. Their success led to a record deal and millions of dollars in royalties, but Brian found that even after all they had achieved together, it didn't fulfill him in the way he thought it would. "My dream came true ... I made more money. I played bigger shows. I had houses and cars. I tried everything to try and get pleasure out of this life. And I thought that I could fulfill my life with all this stuff by having my dream come true. And it came true, but it didn't fulfill it."[11]

We repeatedly see this phenomenon in people who reach success expecting to experience the promised land of happiness but find that something is still missing. We should recognize this as a warning sign and reevaluate our own personal journeys; so that we don't continue to perpetuate the unhappiness epidemic in our country. The time has come for us to break out of the habit of pursuing enjoyment based on the belief that once we have (*blank*), then we will be happy.

Many have bought into the belief that they will accomplish whatever happiness that they feel is missing from their lives once they retire. They set their sights on retirement as the ideal lifestyle providing the time and money to do whatever one wants to do—a recipe certain to produce happiness. Once we have that level of freedom, it will allow us to pursue happy experiences every day for the rest of our life. That was what Michael Phelps thought he was going to do, and it's what most of us look forward to doing. Many people can't wait to walk away from their jobs and travel the world, learn a new hobby, or play more golf. The goal of early retirement has become the new American Dream, but it didn't start out that way.

In 1935, the US government created the Social Security Act, which would provide a pension plan for workers to retire starting at age sixty-five so they could make room for younger, more productive workers. The life expectancy at birth that year was just sixty years old.[12] Many of the workers didn't want to stop working when they had reached that age. In fact, the concept of retirement was still so unpopular in 1951 that Corning Corporation created a group of scholars to research and help "educate" aging individuals into enjoying leisure activities. They decided they needed "a major effort designed to glamorize leisure as we have not." Shortly after that, insurance companies joined in and began a national campaign to sell the public on the idea of retirement as the new American Dream.[13]

This marketing campaign coincided with the golden age of consumerism in America. The country had just come out of World War II, which had helped pull America out of the Great Depression from all the military spending. But with the war over, there was a fear the economy might enter another recession. Corporations became more sophisticated in their marketing during this time and created a new narrative that made consumerism patriotic. Historian Lizabeth Cohen described it like this: "The good purchaser devoted to *'more, newer, and better'* was the good citizen." Companies even tied people's sense of self-worth and their standing in society to the products they purchased.[14]

To this day, we can still see the effectiveness of those campaigns. Leisure is the preferred way to spend our free time. We have not only bought into the idea that retirement is the pinnacle of a successful career but also that the acquisition of things along the way is necessary to living a happy life. We have fallen into a trance, orchestrated by marketers, that has us believing we can find happiness just on the other side of where we are. Every day they bombard us with advertisements consistently showing what we need—fancier cars, more vacations, better clothes, the latest diet. The boom of social media influencers has taken this to another level. We see our peers and our idols doing things we love and sharing products we must have. All of this has a profound impact on our perceived path to happiness. It's time we question the narrative we are being sold and realize the profound effect it is having on us.

DIMINISHING RETURNS

There is an economic principle we learned in high school that plays into this culture of consumerism. It's called *"the law of diminishing marginal utility."* In economics, they define the term "utility" as the amount of satisfaction one receives from consuming a good or service. The law doesn't focus on the satisfaction level between different goods or services but instead on consuming the same one repeatedly. It states that the utility received from each additional unit consumed decreases over time, meaning you get less satisfaction the more you go through.

We have all experienced or witnessed this firsthand throughout our life. Take, for example, our favorite dessert. The first serving of that dessert after dinner is sublime. In fact, it's so good we go for another one and then maybe decide we are content—or maybe not. What happens if we continue to eat serving after serving of that same dessert? By the time we reach our seventh helping, we would not be enjoying it as much as we did with our first one; we might even get sick at some point. That is the law of diminishing marginal utility. And although that is a simple and obvious example, it applies to everything in our lives we consume. A critical factor behind our perpetual search for more is that we are continuously draining the enjoyment out of things in our lives, which is perpetuated by the two fundamental motivations psychologists say we were born with—the desire for pleasure and the avoidance of pain.

Psychological hedonism is a school of thought that believes one of these two emotions drives all our actions. It states that human behavior is based on the desire to seek the things that bring us pleasure and avoid those that bring us pain.[15] When we were children, these drives served as an effective mechanism for learning how to behave in the world. If we avoided doing wrong (and thus avoided the pain of repercussions) and did what our parents told us to (which may have resulted in the pleasure of being praised), we accomplished this core aim. However, these primary motivations can grow into a self-destructive pattern if we seek pleasure regardless of the painful consequences that may result, or avoid pain irrespective of the pleasure it could lead to—for example, choosing to ditch class to hang with our friends or abandoning our adult responsibilities to go on a weekend bender. Seeking pleasure and avoiding pain influence our behavior exponentially when combined with a desire for instant gratification: the need to have, do, and accomplish what we want, right now.

Most of us grow up and learn how to practice delayed gratification as we mature and take control of our impulses. We program ourselves to put the desires for pleasure and avoidance of pain in check, often just by sheer willpower. Yet, these desires persist and are kept alive by our cultural influence to idolize happiness. What if we were to challenge these core longings and replace the drive for pleasure and the avoidance of pain with a more sustaining motivation? Phelps's story shows these internal influences at work, but it also reveals a more profound inspiration that has the potential to truly fulfill us—the desire to live a life of significance and contribute meaningfully to the world.

The pursuit of purpose is the exact opposite of pursuing happiness. Not because it makes us unhappy—far from it—but because it shifts our focus from being all about us to looking at what impact we can have on someone else. When we discover God created us for a purpose, it gives us a new outlook on life. Instead of taking fate into our own hands and looking to our level of emotional happiness as a guide, we will look to the purpose He has instilled within us and the impact it can have on the world. The desire for self-gratification fades into the background and is replaced by the desire to make a meaningful difference in someone else's life. This altruistic attitude imbues us with a sense of worth and value that is not tied to our emotions as we recognize the opportunity we have to serve a greater calling.

Everyone's pursuit of purpose will be unique to them and may even change depending on the various stages of life we find ourselves in. But the foundation that we need to build upon is the same—recognizing the power, source, and mindset that will prepare us for the new journey ahead. Once we establish that, we can explore the building blocks found within the design of our own lives that will point us to the specific expression of purpose we were created to share with the world.

Breaking out of our status quo and experiencing lasting fulfillment starts by contemplating this question: "What if my life has a deeper meaning beyond what I am currently living for?" Choosing to start this new journey means we must throw out the old system used to evaluate our life by exchanging our tape measure of happiness for a scale that weighs our purpose. In other words, we will no longer base all our decisions on what will make us happy; but rather contemplate how we can address a problem or need in someone's life to best help them. This new means of measurement will point us in a different direction and produce a level of satisfaction within us that goes beyond any feelings of happiness and into the realm of joy and true fulfillment.

Joy may seem like a synonym for happiness, but it's a different experience entirely, in actuality. When we have joy, it's not dependent on our circumstances or anything external. It's a reflection of our internal frame of mind that focuses on something more significant. We can be in the darkest of situations and still have deep-rooted joy if it's found in something greater than ourselves. The circumstances we face will then no longer determine the level of satisfaction we experience. Purpose can give us the power to discover such true fulfillment that will change our lives. As we will explore next, embracing this is the first step to building the foundation of our new journey.

2

THE POWER

"Perhaps the single most important ingredient in all of life for achieving happiness and fulfillment: Purpose"

—HARVEY VOLSON

One of my earliest childhood memories was in third grade when I met my first crush. I did everything I could to display my affection for her, yet she wasn't interested. As I got older, this became a recurring pattern in my life—I would meet someone I really liked, and the start of a relationship appeared hopeful, yet it would end in heartbreak. In high school, I started drinking with friends and going to parties, which exaggerated my emotions and made my feelings more volatile. The trail of broken relationships that followed left me feeling alone and exposed an inner void—something was missing in my life.

During the winter of my sophomore year, I came across *The Purpose Driven Life* by Rick Warren, and the premise intrigued me. As I started reading it, my perspective changed. I learned for the first time that my life had meaning and purpose beyond trying to be happy. The book offered an invitation to live for something bigger, which soothed the inner longings I had been wrestling with. I suddenly was less concerned with finding a girlfriend as I realized God had allowed me to experience these painful feelings to prepare me for something greater. This revelation gave me an entirely new perspective on my life.

But it didn't take long for a sense of guilt to wash over me. My lifestyle of drinking and partying felt completely out of line with what I assumed would please God. Wanting to rid myself of the feelings of condemnation, I decided to forget about everything I had just learned and trade my guilt for what felt much better in the present moment. Despite reverting to my old way of looking at life, this brief encounter with God had planted a seed of purpose within me.

The pattern of "love sought, love lost" continued to repeat itself each year in high school as I longed for a romantic connection that would satiate my soul. Each experience left a searing wound within my heart. It culminated during spring break my senior year in Daytona Beach. I met the girl of my dreams the first day I arrived and spent the week hanging out with her. We were together every day as I got to know her and her family. When the blissful week ended, we had to return home—she headed back to North Carolina while I returned to Chicago.

I was crushed. Finally, I met someone with a mutual interest, but the hope of being together disappeared as we returned home to reality. Emotionally wrecked, I started to question everything and fell into a victim mentality: Why does this always happen to me? Why do I always have these painful feelings? What is the point of life anyway? Why am I even here? I hated feeling the pain of these emotions that I could never control. I became depressed and numb to everything around me. I was lost, confused, and fed up—completely apathetic toward life.

After graduation, I headed off to school at the University of Iowa. I never answered the questions surrounding my heartbreak but instead sucked it up and moved on. I stuffed away the feelings that hurt and looked forward to the next chapter of my life. Two months into school, I met a man named Rory, who was on campus helping college kids start their own online businesses. I wasn't really interested at first, but the opportunity to make money was compelling. After a lot of thought, my friend Matt and I decided to get started working with him.

Our business grew rather quickly, and Rory invited us to a weekend conference to learn from other leaders in the organization. I was excited to glean some wisdom from them and apply it to my business to make more money. On the last day of the conference, they had a Sunday morning service before the final lineup of speakers began. I went along, not fully knowing what to expect. After a few songs played, one of the leaders got on stage and shared their personal struggles and how they had discovered a void or missing piece in their life that was only satisfied in knowing Jesus.

Wait a minute, was I in church? I was speechless. I felt a rush of emotions as I recalled how I turned my back on God a few years ago. Despite my efforts to run away, God pursued me. In that moment, I was convicted of my sin and the way I was living. I asked God to forgive me and vowed that day to commit my life to following Jesus. I suddenly felt whole and complete as tears of compassion fell down my cheek. A sense of peace washed over me and soothed my deepest longings. It finally hit me square in the face—God was what I had been searching for this entire time. He was what had been missing in my life. I became charged with energy at this call to step into his purpose for me.

Returning to campus, my outlook on life had changed wholly and undoubtedly. The wound in my heart slowly mended. I quit drinking shortly after that and no longer desired to party every chance I got. I gave up my fixation on trying to find a girlfriend. In place of that, I started reading the Bible and other books that helped me grow personally and professionally. I became energized at the chance to help others discover that they, too, were created for a purpose bigger than themselves. This epiphany became a turning point of my life—and the start of a new journey to follow God and help other people as I embraced the purpose for which I was created.

The discovery that my life had meaning and significance empowered me to drastically change the way I lived. I tried to do all that I could to live with happiness as I searched for a girlfriend and drank with my friends. But that pursuit just left me feeling worse off—I was depressed, lost, and had very low self-esteem. This inner void I had that something was missing continued to grow deeper until God showed me that my life had a purpose. The power of this new truth allowed me to step out of my old way of living. I gained a fresh perspective that gave me the strength to see the purpose in the challenging moments I encountered and how they were preparing me for something greater.

I firmly believe when we discover that we were created for a reason beyond just living to be happy, it can positively influence our behavior and change the way we look at our life. It provides a new outlook that affects everything we do. Instead of focusing on our pleasure or all that we can acquire, we look for how we can impact the world. This leads to greater fulfillment and resiliency as we live for something bigger than ourselves. When we believe our lives are full of purpose, it changes our perspective and gives us a new framework for making decisions.

THE POWER TO CHANGE OUR PERSPECTIVE

During his 1961 inauguration speech, John F. Kennedy famously said, "My fellow Americans, ask not what your country can do for you—ask what you can do for your country." Kennedy's call to change our perspective from asking what we can get to asking what we can give is what purpose is all about. This allows us to change our view from looking in the mirror every day and thinking about ourselves to looking out the window to see what meaning our life has out there. What value can I bring to the world instead of what value can I attain for myself? Realizing that our life has the most significance, not in what we can acquire but rather in what we can share, is a complete paradigm shift we are all capable of making.

This new perspective allows us to see things we couldn't see before. Our focus changes; we become less concerned with what will maximize our happiness and instead intrigued to find out the reason our lives exist. The meaning and significance behind why we are alive brings us to ask questions that we may not have thought to ask before. As we journey to answer those questions, it will alter the way in which we look at everything. It changes the lens through which we view the world and make decisions by zooming out to see the bigger picture of our lives. Instead of just living for the weekend or our next vacation, we can choose to expand our perspective by considering how our actions today will have an impact five or ten years from now.

When I learned that God created me for a purpose, it gave me a completely new outlook on the duration of life. I had been living with the viewpoint that only looked out from week to week as I sought to maximize my enjoyment. Yet, I didn't think much about what would happen five years down the road, or even further, after I passed away someday. My frame of mind was very short-term and limited to life on this earth. Changing my perspective opened my eyes to the realization that our lives have unlimited potential to serve others and leave a legacy. The decisions we make now have the potential to leave a lasting impact on future generations to come.

We can expand our perspective by asking ourselves: who will remember us when we are gone? What will they remember us for? Those questions point our focus to the current impact we are having and allow us to consider the ways purpose empowers us to live differently. If these questions about life are hard or scary to answer, that is okay. They were difficult for me to consider at first. It made me think long and hard about how my actions today would play out down the road. The power purpose has in our lives is unlocked as our outlook changes. When we think in terms of the legacy we will leave, it will embolden us to make different decisions and have a new attitude.

This shift in mindset has a direct impact on our self-worth. We can often equate the value of something to its usefulness or cost to produce. When we expand our perspective to look at the world and our lives with a zoomed-out view, the understood value of our lives increases. We recognize the priceless worth we were created with and see the new applications our life has to offer others. The usefulness of a screwdriver pales in comparison to a Swiss Army knife. Not only does the Swiss Army knife possess the screwdriver as one of its functions, but it also has about thirteen other uses. The pursuit of happiness is much like that screwdriver—it has one function. But purpose is like the Swiss Army knife—it has multiple uses and applications. As we realize the value our lives hold, we will begin to look for the impact we can have in the world, just like Blake Mycoskie did.

During a vacation to Argentina one year, Blake noticed a great need—so many kids there didn't have shoes. That simple clothing item prohibited them from going to school and getting an education since shoes were part of a required school dress code. Moved by this level of poverty, he thought about what he could do to help. At the same time, he grew an affinity for the style of shoes offered for sale in Argentina. An idea came to him to take these locally made shoes and sell them in the US, but with a twist—for every pair of shoes sold, he would give one away to a child in need.

In 2006, Blake founded the TOMS shoe company. This novel business model, which came to be known as the "one-for-one concept," grew into a great success. By adding a more prudent purpose behind each shoe that was sold, it created significantly more value than one without it. Customers were able to not only buy shoes they liked but were able to have an impact by helping kids who couldn't afford to get their own. This new business model became widely popular, and other companies started to spring up using the same idea with different products. Adding a bigger purpose to these products multiplied their value. By focusing on giving shoes away for free, TOMS ended up having more sales than they could have ever imagined.[16]

When we realize we have a greater purpose of giving and serving others, our usefulness expands, increasing our perceived value. The fact that our lives hold such potential proves that we have intrinsic merit. It reveals the natural gifts, talents, and abilities we have to help those around us. We see opportunities to impact others positively, as looking for purpose gives us a new perspective to see meaning in places we never saw before. This not only grows our self-worth but also increases our resiliency. It unlocks one of the most powerful components of purpose—the ability to preserve through whatever life throws at us.

THE POWER TO OVERCOME OUR CIRCUMSTANCES

The most powerful difference purpose can have, is its ability to enable us to transcend our circumstances. When we encounter an unbearable situation, such as the death of a loved one, an illness, or sudden job loss, we can easily lose our happiness. If that is the only thing we are living for, then we become derailed by the trauma in our lives and can easily fall into despair. But, recognizing our purpose allows us to overcome our circumstances. It creates in us an attitude that is not affected by the various challenges we face. This produces a satisfaction that is not derived from what happens to us.

If our primary motives in life are to pursue pleasure and avoid pain, we will inevitably be disappointed because life has particular unavoidable sufferings. But when our primary motivation shifts to living with purpose, we have a brand-new outlook that can guide us through the trauma we face in life. We still feel the pain and the heaviness, but our search for meaning provides something bigger to live for in those moments. Having a focus on our purpose can help us survive even the gravest circumstances.

In 1942, during the rise of the Nazi regime across eastern Europe, Viktor Frankl—an Austrian psychologist—along with his parents, wife, and brother, were all detained and thrown into a concentration camp. Over the next three years, all his family members died either by sickness or extermination. Viktor remained in Auschwitz and eventually came down with typhoid fever. He ultimately survived by his determination to rewrite a manuscript of a book he had started before being imprisoned. He developed a psychological theory from his experience that those who possessed "the will to meaning" had the best chance of survival in the camps. "The lesson one could learn from Auschwitz," he says, "and in other concentration camps, in the final analysis, was, those who were oriented toward a meaning—toward a meaning to be fulfilled by them in the future—were most likely to survive."[17]

Viktor had everything taken away from him and endured the most inhumane treatment. Being left with nothing would have made it very easy for him to fall into despair and surrender to his demise. His situation was exceedingly dire, yet he knew his life still had purpose. He found a meaning to live for despite all he had lost. In his book *Man's Search for Meaning* (the very one he had vowed to himself to finish), he summed it up best as: "A man who becomes conscious of the responsibility he bears toward a human being who affectionately waits for him, or to an unfinished work, will never be able to throw away his life. He knows the 'why' for his existence and will be able to bear almost any 'how.'"

THE POWER TO CHANGE OUR LIFE

Living for a purpose greater than ourselves has the power to change our lives. As you think about that, what areas of your life could this shift in focus really make a difference in? Where do you usually turn your attention when you are struggling or facing challenges? How might your life change if you were to realize that God was calling you to something bigger?

Thinking about these questions may only be a seed planted that will take years to grow and develop as it did for me. But spending the time to investigate and find a more compelling reason to live will be well worth it. If we are to discover a purpose that is greater than ourselves, we must look beyond our own lives to see that we are being called to something greater. Our perspective needs to shift from focusing on what we can get out of life and instead look toward what we have that can help others. That may sound good now, but when hardships and challenges come our way, we can easily lose sight of this new focus and fall back into survival mode by seeking to ease our pain at all costs.

That was certainly true in my experience on more than one occasion. We can go to any length to numb our pain when we face stressful challenges or overwhelming circumstances. If life gets bad enough, it can feel like we are being swallowed up, unable to think about anything other than the present trauma we are facing. Apathy can set in and become paralyzing. That was what I felt my senior year of high school after so many devastating heartbreaks. If you ever find yourself there, one of the first things to realize is that it's okay to feel that way, but those experiences don't have to define your life. We can look for a deeper purpose to help us overcome our challenging situations. After losing almost everything, Viktor Frankl concluded after his time in the concentration camps that "Life is never made unbearable by circumstances, but only by lack of meaning and purpose."

Whatever you are currently facing, or may someday face in the future, I want you to consider this possibility—what if God is preparing you for something bigger? What if you are going through this painful situation so that one day you can help someone else who is going through the same thing? Perhaps right now, you are acquiring the life experience needed to relate and help others navigate the same challenge. This becomes a profound purpose you can look to that only you will be able to fulfill. When we believe our life has greater meaning than just trying to be happy, it will empower us to look beyond our current circumstances to live for the bigger purpose it holds.

As we lay the first part of our foundation with this new attitude, we need to be mindful of the sources we are deriving meaning from in our lives. If we look in the wrong area, we can end up relying on finding purpose on things that are conditional—which will only leave us vulnerable to disappointment. Next, we are going to explore the various sources of purpose and identify one that will establish a solid foundation we can trust.

3

THE SOURCE

———

"The two most important days in life are the day
you are born and the day you find out why."

—MARK TWAIN

At the age of eighteen, Katie Davis Majors moved to Jinja, Uganda, and founded a nonprofit called Amazima Ministries International. Her mission was to educate, empower, and encourage the orphaned, poor, and vulnerable in the country of Uganda. Over the past decade, under Katie's leadership, they have enrolled eight hundred kids in school, provided 17,500 people with medical care, and served over two million meals. The same year Katie started this ministry, she also began fostering Ugandan children within the surrounding community. By the time she was twenty-three years old, Katie had become the mother of thirteen girls in the process of officially adopting them.[18]

In her book *Kisses from Katie*, she explains, "I would like to say my ministry was born out of a carefully thought-out plan. These things simply aren't true, though. I was walking through life one moment at a time, blown away by what God could do through me if I simply said yes." Her remarkable journey wasn't the result of extensive planning or a lifelong goal to start a nonprofit. Katie's faith was her source of purpose in life, and the journey she found herself on was simply the result of being committed to her beliefs. Deciding to do all of this at such a young age had its challenges, but Katie couldn't have been more fulfilled. She found her purpose in meeting the needs of children on the other side of the world.

It all started in Brentwood, Tennessee, where Katie grew up living a very typical, suburban life. She was the homecoming queen at her high school and had plans to go off to college after graduation to study nursing. In her free time, Katie volunteered for a homeless shelter in Nashville, which eventually led her to look for places to serve outside of the country before starting college. She applied to several different international trips for her senior year winter break and chose an organization in Uganda because they were the first to respond.

Within her first few days of arriving in Uganda, Katie was moved with compassion for the people, the country, and the overwhelming amount of poverty she encountered. It was unlike anything she had ever seen before. After the winter break trip ended, she learned of an opportunity to teach English at a kindergarten school in an orphanage for children in the town she had visited. Katie didn't have any experience teaching but was excited to go back and serve the community in Uganda for a whole year before starting college.

Katie's first day teaching in the classroom at the school was very overwhelming. There were 140 kids in the kindergarten class all staring at her, amazed at how different her skin color was. Katie's attempts to greet them were met with wide-eyed stares as they didn't speak any English. As the weeks went by, she got to know the students better. But then she noticed something strange—several of the kids stopped showing up.

It turned out their parents could no longer afford the minimal amount the school was charging for tuition. Sometimes, families even abandoned their kids at the orphanage so they would receive food and schooling because they didn't have the means to support them.

Katie's heart broke at this realization of the devastating effect poverty was having on these families. She thought about possible solutions in which these children could remain with their parents and still attend school. She called and emailed her friends and family back home to share the story of what was happening in Uganda. Katie explained how it cost less than a dollar a day to provide tuition, food, and medical care for one child at the school—a small amount of money to keep these families together. Through her conviction and the generosity of people close to her, they raised enough to provide a year's worth of care for ten kids.

Shortly after that, those ten students on scholarship turned into forty, which turned into a hundred—and eventually, Amazima was born. The ministry quickly snowballed, and Katie needed to find an office location in order to register as a nonprofit. She moved out of the orphanage and started looking for a house to live and run the ministry from. There weren't many homes available to rent, and the one she found that was available happened to be much larger than what she really needed.

Not long after moving, a house in town collapsed on a young nine-year-old girl named Agnes, leaving her and her two younger siblings homeless. Katie found out they didn't have any parents or relatives still alive. These three girls—ages nine, seven, and five—were all alone to care for themselves. Heartbroken at the news, Katie offered to have them come stay with her until they could find a family in the community to take care of them. After several weeks of looking, God confirmed to Katie that she was the family these girls were searching for and began the fostering process. She never set out with an intention to adopt children but eventually welcomed these kids to become a permanent part of her family.

Katie started the long adoption process and, at the end of the school year in Uganda, returned to Nashville to visit her parents. She had promised them before she left that she would go off to college, but the thought of that now made her feel like she was turning her back on what God was calling her to do in Uganda. A terribly uncomfortable feeling overcame her as she was suddenly back living in American culture. The contrast was striking compared to the extreme poverty she had lived among for the past year, leaving her feeling very unsettled. It became clear to her that Uganda was not a one-year thing—it was a lifetime commitment.

After many conversations with her parents, she bought a one-way ticket back to Uganda and returned to her new home to continue to grow her ministry and help the families in the community. "I'm not here to eliminate poverty, to eradicate disease, to put a stop to people abandoning babies," Katie says. "God reminded me again that day that I have one purpose, in Uganda and in life, and that is to love."[19]

There were many things Katie could have looked to for purpose in her life—getting into a good college, graduating with honors, working in the medical field, and caring for her family back home. All of those might have led her to fulfill expressions of meaning; but, before looking for specific ways to live out her purpose, she first turned her attention to the source of purpose in her life for guidance. Instead of starting with a plan for how to have an impact on the world, Katie focused on her faith and belief in God for what to do. In the end, this led her to a bigger, more fulfilling calling than she could have found on her own.

There are plenty of things we can look to in our lives that give us purpose. At times it may even be confusing to decipher between them as they compete for our attention. We can find meaning in growing to become a better person, working hard to get a promotion, getting good grades, or learning something new to accomplish a bucket list goal. In fact, we can even look at happiness as the reason behind why we do things. The reality is we can find purpose all around us. To live with meaning that leads to true fulfillment, we need to look at the source of purpose that will shape our thoughts and decisions. It is paramount that we build upon a foundation that can actually fulfill us instead of one that will merely leave us searching for more.

THE SOURCE OF STRIFE

Golf was a huge part of my life growing up, thanks to the influence of my dad, who was a PGA instructor. I had my first set of clubs when I was two years old. As high school approached, I made it my goal to earn a spot on the varsity golf team when I was a freshman. I practiced almost every day, working on all aspects of my golf game to prepare for tryouts. This singular focus was the purpose behind spending hours and hours at the driving range, working with swing coaches, and perfecting my short game. It was the reason behind all of my decisions about how I spent my free time. My hard work paid off as I qualified for the varsity team my freshman year, but my drive to accomplish more didn't end once I reached that goal.

I was thrilled with my achievement, but once I made the varsity team, I set my sights on a new aspiration: to be the number one player on the team. My identity became rooted in becoming a great golfer. There was never an end to my striving because the goal kept changing. My mood would fluctuate along with how well I had played that day. And my sense of self-worth became tied to whether I won or lost. The frustrating thing with the game of golf is—you can always do better. There is always at least one shot you could have hit better, no matter how well you played that day. This self-destructive attitude of never being good enough develops when our measure for evaluating ourselves is constantly changing.

The pursuit of happiness is, by its very nature, set up the same way—the source we look to is ourselves, driven by what we think will make us happy. Our desires become the focal point that determines what we will do or acquire to bring us enjoyment. But it is an unreliable source that is constantly changing due to the volatility of our desires; as they fluctuate, so does that which will make us happy. This overemphasis on ourselves can also negatively impact our interactions with others.

Looking to our happiness for guidance leads us to base our actions on a desire to be accepted, liked, or approved of by others. It's human nature to want to connect with other people, but when our focus is constantly on how we feel, we tend to make it our aim to make sure everyone likes us. It's not always as apparent as it might seem, but this can become a path to misery. Being kind to others and caring for people can be a rewarding act of love, but doing it out of a desire to win their approval and acceptance can turn it into a source of strife.

We can trace the root of this back to selfishness. The dictionary defines the word "selfishness" as "the lack of consideration for others; concerned chiefly with one's own personal profit or pleasure." When we are operating from selfish motivation, even the greatest pursuits of purpose will not be fulfilling to us because our source of guidance will still be our own pleasure and happiness. We will continue our striving as we seek to control the outcome of our interactions with others. In order to find fulfillment in the pursuit of purpose, we need to give up this motivation attached to the end results.

That can be hard to do when we are trained from a young age to be very outcome-driven based on the way we measure success. Doing well in school is measured by our grades, excelling in sports is measured by winning, and flourishing in life is measured by our happiness. We have become conditioned to place the success of any given endeavor on the outcome we attain. But if we take this same mentality into our journey to find purpose, we will just end up adding something new to chase after. If we are to experience the fulfillment found in the pursuit of purpose, we can't just set a new goal for ourselves to accomplish.

There is nothing wrong with setting goals to grow and become better—in fact, by themselves, they are a healthy component of our lives. But when these goals become our primary focus and source of purpose, we set ourselves up to constantly strive for more. Putting our focus on these outcomes takes our minds off the present moment as we become consumed with trying to accomplish them. Goals are not a sustainable source of purpose in our lives because they are constantly changing. They have this illusion that they will be all satisfying, but upon accomplishing them, we then look for the next one to shoot for—the next bigger, bolder one to achieve. At the end of the day, they are all limited in their capacity to fulfill us because they are never constant.

It's common for people to hear a story like Katie's and become inspired to follow in her footsteps—to make a big difference in the world and have a meaningful impact by setting a goal to create a massive organization and bring about change in developing countries like she did. Wouldn't that lead to a tremendous impact with a sustainable purpose in our lives? It might, but it also might not. The better question to ask is how did Katie get there? It wasn't by being fixated on the end result or by putting it on her vision board of new year's resolutions. It was by being present in that moment to honor her faith and live out her beliefs one decision at a time.

Being present in each moment will allow us to find purpose that is truly sustaining. We need to maintain this state of equilibrium to keep our balance. The scientific term for this is "homeostasis," meaning "a steady state of internal conditions." When we seek to attain a purpose that is outside of ourselves, it is not sustainable. It breaks our equilibrium and shifts our focus on what we don't have instead of that which we do. That requires us to become someone we are not to reach our desired outcome. Striving to live someone else's journey of purpose will wear us out. But if we look to the God-given purpose within us and the call He placed upon our heart, that can sustain us. There isn't something external that we need to accomplish first—it's already present within us. When we look to the manufacturer of our souls, we discover a powerful source of purpose that reveals our lives were created with meaning and significance that is our responsibility to steward.

The difference we are invited into when we read Katie's story is not that we need to set a new goal to find our calling in the world, but that we need to start by connecting to the greater source of purpose that is within us. What if God intentionally created each of us for a specific mission? If that is true, our efforts to search for meaning in life should begin with following the unique design of our lives for clues of this purpose. By looking at our personality, talents, and abilities, we must ask ourselves how we came to be this way. Is it just by chance that we possess the qualities that we do, or is there a reason behind the uniqueness of our lives that will lead us to a higher purpose?

THE SUPERNATURAL SOURCE

Since the beginning of time, civilizations have sought to find answers to explain the origin of life and why we exist. They have looked at the stars for clues, erected objects of worship thought to possess power, and named gods after the elements in the world they couldn't explain. Advances in modern science have allowed further study into understanding our world at a deeper level for more clues. But even the most outstanding scientists on the planet can't explain the theory of how living things were created from an explosion of non-living matter; the specific elements that had to be perfect, in order to sustain life at that moment, rule out "chance" as a possible explanation.

An article entitled "Science Finds God" published in *Newsweek* discusses this exact phenomenon:

"It turns out that if the constants of nature—unchanging numbers like the strength of gravity, the charge of an electron, and the mass of a proton—were the tiniest bit different, then atoms would not hold together, stars would not burn and life would never have made an appearance. 'When you realize that the laws of nature must be incredibly finely tuned to produce the universe we see,' says John Polkinghorne, a former physicist at Cambridge University, 'That conspires to plant the idea that the universe did not just happen, but that there must be a purpose behind it.'"

Scientists have a hypothesis to speculate on the origin of life, but it remains a mystery to many. Attempts to recreate the big bang in laboratories have failed to result in creating life. This unexplainable realm points to the supernatural—something not of our universe, which has the power to manifest life from nothing. This is the realm of faith, and it invites us to consider the possibility that there is an all-powerful God who created earth and life as we know it with purpose.

"God is not just the starting point of your life; he is the *source* of it," says Rick Warren, author of *The Purpose Driven Life*. "When God made you, he wired you in a certain way and uniquely shaped you for a contribution. Nobody has been you in the past or will be you in the future. God doesn't create clones or copies. God didn't create anything without a purpose. If you're breathing, you have a purpose ... you have something to offer the world."

There is purpose all around us, but it is the meaning within us that truly holds the ability to produce a fulfilling life. The ambition we inherently contain, rather than the external purposes that we are enticed to pursue. When we look at the uniqueness of our lives, we see that there is a reason behind our existence. We were uniquely created with passions and talents that are the source of tremendous purpose. They point to the meaning our lives contain, without us becoming something we are not, in order to find it. God gave us a purpose when he created us the exact way that he did. Just like any inventor can tell you the best application of their invention, God knows best when it comes to the purpose that will actually sustain us.

When was the last time you asked yourself: what is the reason for doing the things I do? Or where do I look to find purpose in life? Let's take a moment to think about some of our roles and activities so that we can reflect on the motivations currently driving us. By turning our awareness to identify where we naturally look to find purpose, we can discern if it is from a place of fulfillment or striving—something internal or external to our identity. There is a simple question you can ask yourself to get to the root of what is currently driving your life: *why? Why* do you work where you do? *Why* do you have the hobbies that you do? *Why* do you do everything that you do?

This simple question will uncover the sources we are looking to for purpose in our life. Is the answer tied to a particular outcome we wish to get; or a grander purpose rooted in our identity that we feel created to do? As we think about that question, we can then decide if we need to replace the source of our purpose with something bigger by connecting to the one who intentionally formed our lives.

This leads us to the final element of our foundation that we will solidify in the next chapter—having the mindset that realizes it's a journey about living life *with* purpose; instead of living *for* it.

4

THE MINDSET

———

"The purpose of life is a life of purpose."

—ROBERT BYRNE

When I turned twenty-one, I started an annual tradition on New Year's Day where I would spend the entire day setting goals. I would reflect and journal on the year that had just concluded and write out my goals for the year ahead. I summarized my intentions for the upcoming year on a giant whiteboard in my bedroom as a daily reminder—something I still do to this day. But what I didn't know at the time was how this habit would eventually lead to one of the biggest crises of my life.

My twenties could easily be defined as my "grind" period. I was on a mission to get to a place of success and accomplishment with school, work, and finance. Amid setting goals, I had learned the importance of having a singleness of purpose. A source of motivation that fueled the drive to accomplish the goals that I had. This singular focus became the reason for everything I did: "To use the resources that God has given me to build a strong, prosperous, God-centered family that will better God's kingdom."

I wasn't married or dating anyone seriously, but this vision for a family was something I sincerely wanted someday. It became such a strong passion that it shaped my career decision and inspired me to work extremely hard. I aimed to get to a place where I could comfortably provide for my future family. I never set a certain age by which I wanted to accomplish this, mainly because at twenty-one, you feel like you have all the time in the world.

The way I approached accomplishing this vision was tied to my favorite subject in school: math. I liked it because there was only one right solution, and if you simply followed the formula, you got the correct answer. This became the lens through which I also viewed obtaining my goals. If $x + y = z$, then in order for me to get z, all I need to do is figure out x and y. In other words, achieving my desired outcome was simply a function of what I put into it. Good grades required paying attention in class and dedicated study time—add those two ingredients together, and I will get good grades.

With this mindset, I accomplished my goals over the next nine years. I finished school at the top of my class, got an incredible job, bought a house, went on amazing mission trips, and was dating, hoping to find a wife—but something happened as I was about to exit my twenties. The flame that had been the driving force within me slowly faded. The last goal that had been the source of my purpose had yet to happen—I was still single. I questioned for the first time if I was ever going to meet someone or if maybe I was going to be alone forever.

With my thirtieth birthday just months away, all the hope I had for my future turned to despair. I wasn't dating anyone seriously and had no future family in sight. I realized I had this subconscious expectation that I would already be married and starting a family by the time I turned thirty. Unlike my other accomplishments in life, the simple mathematical formula here wasn't working. Talking to girls and going on dates didn't inevitably lead me to the outcome I had hoped. My identity began to unravel. The vision I had for living out my purpose by selflessly loving my wife and raising children that would impact the world for God seemed like a distant dream. My motivation for life shriveled up and depression set in. I felt lost, scared, and alone.

That led me to start talking to a counselor. I found one through my church and scheduled the next available meeting. I sat down in Andy's office on my first visit and, out of my grief, shared the core issue I was wrestling with: "I want to do something great with my life, to live with purpose and impact, to leave a legacy; and sometimes I struggle with what that is, what that looks like, or if I'm even capable." I explained to him my driving motivation to have a God-centered family and how turning thirty brought about a crisis as I felt purposeless from my missed expectations.

After months of talking with Andy, I discovered something profound. I had been using a scorecard to evaluate myself based solely on my results. It seemed reasonable to do since that is how I accomplished the other goals in my life. I felt in control by simply plugging in the right pieces to the formula: $x + y = z$. But I wasn't getting the answer I wanted. The more I focused on the desired outcome, the more anxiety and fear I experienced, as my scorecard reflected failure. I realized this motivation that had been driving me until now was entirely out of my control and needed to change.

I had to replace the way that I measured my results by finding something else to evaluate. Something that gave me inspiration and excitement that was within my control. Andy and I started to talk about being authentic. What if I based my success on if I authentically showed up, regardless of the outcome? This discussion gave me a lot of energy, and I thought about other values I had that I could focus on, such as love, connection, and wholeheartedness. Slowly I changed the scorecard to evaluate my success based on my ability to live out these values. If I did, then it didn't matter what the outcome was—it was a win.

I'd like to say that making that change led me to the original results I was hoping for, but it hasn't. I am still very much single, and that's okay. In fact, my thirties have genuinely been the best years of my life. I now have a driving purpose that isn't dependent on my ability to accomplish something or contingent on things that are outside of my control. My new singleness of purpose is *to live out my values for God through a wholehearted, courageous life that loves people and inspires spiritual growth to know Jesus and discover their purpose*. I can live that out right now, regardless of my circumstances.

The difference between my original statement of purpose and the one I arrived at afterward boiled down to my mindset. In the first one, I had built my life around living *for a purpose*, whereas, with this new perspective, I focused on living *with purpose*. It was a subtle difference, which profoundly impacted how I viewed my life, made decisions, and evaluated my success.

When our mindset focuses on a purpose that we don't yet have the ability to express, we set our sights on trying to get it. We reduce living with meaning for just another goal to check off. Our energy goes into trying to attain the role, position, or accomplishment that we think we need to have a meaningful impact on others. Purpose, in this case, can become selfish in that it's really more concerned about getting something for ourselves than giving it to others.

But if we shift our perspective to see that our purpose is already within us, it will allow us to look for the meaning our lives currently hold. We can consider the existing talents and abilities we have and the mission they point us to. Our awareness will then turn to identify the needs of others we are already uniquely equipped to serve. This eliminates the self-centered focus to add something to our lives first or become someone we're not. We then realize there isn't just one path we can take, but that the building blocks of our life can be arranged to display several different expressions of purpose.

LIVING FOR A PURPOSE

LEGOs were a big part of my life growing up. It was on every one of my birthday and Christmas wish lists for several years. I had such a fascination with building things and creating something I could play with by assembling a bunch of random pieces together. Each set came with a book of instructions to follow to produce the finished product displayed on the box—a car, ship, building, etc. Following the instructions took hundreds of pieces and produced one specific outcome. But that isn't the only thing those LEGO pieces could build—the possibilities were really endless. I could arrange the combination of the various building blocks to create whatever my LEGO town needed.

Living *for a purpose* is like trying to follow the LEGO manual's instructions to build something specific. It puts all our focus on the outcome we see on the box and making sure we are careful to do each step correctly. If we miss one or don't follow each step accurately, we will fail, in our eyes, to attain the finished product. It can leave us feeling discouraged as we evaluate our progress based on if we reach this desired outcome or not. This mindset keeps us from seeing the meaning our life has to offer the world right now and how it might change throughout the future.

What may be our purpose in one stage of our life could look a lot different in a new chapter. Life is constantly changing. We are constantly changing. Our passion for pursuing something could mean one thing while we are single and then could radically differ as we enter marriage. If we remain fixed on a singular purpose, it will create a tunnel vision that causes us to miss new opportunities to grow and impact others. There may be an overarching theme that develops from our journey of purpose, but putting it on hold until we reach a certain status, position, or place in life makes it conditional on our efforts to achieve such results.

This mindset causes our meaning and significance to depend on our circumstances. It keeps us from being present and becomes something we will begin *when we get there*. But what if our circumstances never change? What if our marital status, job, or ministry stays exactly the same? Waiting for such things to fall into place first is like leaving the LEGO pieces boxed up until we get enough to build a replica of Chicago. It would be a pretty amazing thing to build, but waiting for it keeps our potential locked up that could be used to start making a difference right now.

Take, for example, accumulating wealth. Let's say we tie our purpose into focusing on achieving some level of financial success in life so that we can then give back and help others. This philanthropic mindset is undoubtably admirable, but what happens if we never attain that success? Does that then mean we have failed our purpose in life? Can we fail to achieve our purpose in life? Is that even possible?

Failure can become a great test by which we evaluate the mentality we have toward purpose in our lives. If we believe that we can fail at accomplishing our purpose, then it is something we are living for instead of something we are living with. How can we fail at something we already possess? It is impossible. The talents, abilities, and experience we currently have are unaffected by failure; because nothing can take those things away from us. They are a part of who we are and independent of our circumstances. The only way we can fail at living with purpose is if we quit looking for it—if we keep these building blocks of our life locked up in a box and stop trying to find the usefulness they hold. But as long as we have the mindset to keep looking, the failures we encounter in life can actually lead us to discover new expressions of purpose.

Spencer Silver learned this principle while he was working for 3M as a research scientist in 1968. He was experimenting in the laboratory to develop a new type of superglue. His job was to create an adhesive that was strong and would hold a solid bond, but Spencer failed to do either of those things. Instead, the glue he ended up creating was extremely weak—so much so that he could easily remove it long after he had set it in place. In his failed attempt at creating a new superglue, Spencer discovered this weak adhesive had a unique property that allowed it to retain its stickiness.[20]

For several years after, he tried to find a use for his failed superglue adhesive, but to no avail. He held seminars in which he shared the unique "microspheres" he had discovered within his glue, which allowed it to remain sticky after its application. His colleagues began to call him "Mr. Persistent" because he wouldn't give up trying to find the purpose for this new adhesive he discovered. Six years after his initial failure, a colleague attended one of his seminars and was later struck with an idea.

Art Fry, who also worked at 3M as a scientist, had been aggravated over a pet peeve he had developed while singing in the church choir. After they were done practicing each Wednesday night, they would mark the page in the hymnals with a small piece of paper to save their place for the upcoming weekend service. But by the time Sunday arrived, the bookmarks had all fallen out. Growing increasingly frustrated, Art remembered Spencer's glue from his seminar and had a eureka moment—Spencer's adhesive could be used to keep the bookmarks in place. That idea led to the creation of the widely popular product, Post-it® Notes.[21]

The glue Spencer set out to create was a complete failure. It was expected to do one thing and totally missed the mark. But amid that perceived failure, it still had usefulness— its purpose was still present. The new glue had a uniqueness that gave it the potential to be used for something specific, which was only realized because Spencer was so determined to find out what it was. The same is true for our lives.

No matter how many times we may experience failure in life, it doesn't change the inherent purpose that we possess. Failure might try to tell us we have missed the mark, but when we look closer, we will realize purpose has been there the whole time. Our lives hold meaning that is waiting to deploy. There is a shift in our thinking that occurs when we discover that truth. We see that it's not about living *for* some common purpose; but rather about living *with* purpose. That's something failure can't take away—we were born with it.

LIVING WITH PURPOSE

It's incredible to think that even with billions of people in the world, no two of us look the same. We were made with the same components—bones, tissues, cells, skin—yet not even identical twins are exactly alike. Each of the body parts we have serves a specific function. All of them, down to the mitochondria of our microscopic cells, have a purpose. They each play a role in allowing us the ability to breathe, think, and move as our brain directs us. If we are to find the purpose each has, we must simply observe their relationship to one another, like how the lungs bring in oxygen to the blood, which gets moved throughout our body by our heart, which—you get the idea.

In the same way, our life has standard building blocks that make up our purpose. We must look at each one to see the relationship between them and the meaning they can collectively display. When we put on the mindset to see that finding purpose starts by looking within our lives, we realize that there is an opportunity to assemble these components to begin expressing purpose right now. We don't have to wait to accomplish anything first. We already hold all the necessary pieces; we just need to break them out of the box and see how they all fit together.

As we do this, we must have the mindset that Spencer did. He didn't know what the purpose of his glue was, but that didn't stop him from exploring its various uses. He spent years relentlessly looking for ways it could be applied and sharing it with others before discovering the purpose it had. When we develop the same mentality, it will enable us to look for the meaning our life holds in any given area—not by searching for something we hope to attain someday, but by looking for the expression of purpose found within the anatomy of our lives.

The defining attribute that will help us maintain the right mindset is determining whether or not we possess the attitude of a servant or that of a tyrant. A servant looks at their life and sees all the ways they can use what they have to be of service to others, whereas the tyrant looks at their life and seeks only to acquire more of what they are missing. There is a simple question we can ask ourselves that will help us have the proper mindset. *In what ways am I uniquely equipped to serve others with my life?* This question keeps our perspective on where it needs to be—focused on what we have and how it might uniquely qualify us to serve something bigger than ourselves. This mindset is key to completing our foundation, which will help us see how the building blocks of our life can impact the world right now.

THE BUILDING BLOCKS OF PURPOSE

We talked about recognizing the power purpose has to change our lives, which helps us see that this journey is more remarkable than any circumstances we face. But to realize that we can't just get our purpose from anywhere, we must consider God as our greater source, which connects us with the story he is inviting us into. When we do, we will see that our purpose is not something we have to wait to express until we arrive at a specific endpoint. We have the potential to contribute to the lives of others from the unique aspects that make us who we are. With that foundation in place, we can identify and assemble the building blocks of purpose to uncover the meaning they hold.

The road ahead is not meant to lead us to a particular destination. Instead, it's meant to launch us on a new journey by changing our awareness. It will help us look at our life differently as we replace our search for happiness with the pursuit of purpose. The fruits of which are not realized in arriving at some particular finish line, but rather in the joy that will inhabit our life along the way. It's not a sprint to power through as fast as possible, but a marathon that will span the course of our lifetime—the effects of which will leave behind a legacy in the hearts and minds of the people we touch along the way.

In the next section, we are going to explore the five common building blocks of purpose. We will look at what we are passionate about, the talents we possess that make us who we are, the painful experiences we've been through, the ability we have to love others, and the opportunities available to us that are unique to our life. Each chapter will highlight a story of someone who demonstrated one of these components and how they found purpose through it. Learning from them will encourage us to piece together the blocks within our own life and discover the purpose they reveal.

Let's begin this journey together to find and live out our purpose.

PART II

THE BUILDING
BLOCKS

5

PASSION: ARE YOU ALIVE?

---

*"If you can't figure out your purpose, figure
out your passion. For your passion will
lead you right into your purpose."*

—T.D. JAKES

If you could do anything in the world and be good at it, what
would you do? If the answer to that question is different from
your current occupation, you're not alone. According to a
survey by MidAmerica Nazarene University, only 25 percent
of Americans say they are currently working in their dream
jobs. Adam Braun, on the other hand, was one of those for-
tunate few who landed his dream job after college. But after
a few years into his career, he became preoccupied with a
different vision—one that would change his life forever.

Adam grew up in the suburbs of New York, surrounded
by several families that worked on Wall Street. He acquired

an obsession with stocks and dreamed of working for an investment firm one day. At the young age of sixteen, he was hired as a summer intern at a hedge fund and was exposed to the lucrative lifestyle within the industry. Captivated by the amount of money he could make, he headed off to Brown University with a clear-cut path to graduate and step into a career on Wall Street.

But, before graduating, Adam signed up to study abroad through the Semester at Sea program. For months he lived on a cruise ship and explored the world while attending classes. On the voyage to the first country, their ship was caught in a terrifying storm while they were eight hundred miles from land. A sixty-foot wave crashed into the boat head-on and shattered the sixth-story windows, flooding the control room and cutting off all power to the engines. The ship was helpless in the middle of the ocean.

As the captain frantically sent out mayday signals and everyone aboard panicked, thoughts raced through Adam's mind. He felt sure that this was going to be the end of his life. Amid the chaos, he recalled some of his fondest memories, which were not any of his possessions or accomplishments, but rather times spent with family and moments helping other people. As his death seemed inevitable, he couldn't help to ask himself why he was put here on this ship to die? What the heck was the point or purpose of his life if it ended right now?

The storm passed, and the ship eventually made it safely to shore. Grateful for having escaped death, Adam felt like he had received a second chance at life. He became determined to make the most of it and not take anything for granted. Adam continued his voyage at sea, intending to answer these new questions about his purpose.

After a few days, they finally arrived in India. It was Adam's first time visiting there, and the level of poverty he witnessed utterly overwhelmed him. The streets were filled with kids begging—some as young as six years old holding babies in their arms asking for money. Adam approached one of the young boys on the street to say hello. As he talked with him, Adam asked this question, "If you could have anything in the world, what would it be?" The boy's response: "A pencil."[22]

That answer shocked Adam—not a house, a toy, or a car—but a pencil? Out of curiosity, he talked further with the boy and realized the wish for a pencil came from the child's desire to go to school. He wanted a chance to learn and study like the other kids his age. This longing resonated deeply with Adam since it was access to education that lifted his parents out of poverty when they moved to America with nothing but the shirts on their backs. Reaching into his backpack, Adam pulled out a pencil to give to the boy, and he instantly illuminated with joy.

The semester eventually ended, and Adam returned to America, a changed person. He had fallen in love with the developing world. He took a full year to travel after graduating college to explore his new passion and answer the lingering questions about what the point of his life was. The year proved to be very fulfilling as Adam solidified his passion for helping kids in the developing world get access to education. Holding onto his dream of working on Wall Street, he decided he could do both. By pursuing a lucrative career, he could accumulate significant wealth and then, in twenty years, be in a financial position to build schools in these communities.

Adam landed his dream job at Bain Capital, setting up his career path into private equity, but he soon realized Wall Street didn't make him come alive the way his trips across the developing world did. Three years into his career, he earned a nine-month sabbatical, and he used it as an opportunity to dive deeper into his passion. He started a nonprofit called Pencils of Promise with twenty-five dollars and a desire to raise just enough money to build one school in the developing world before returning to his job.

But after the sabbatical ended, Adam knew he had found a calling he could not ignore. He spent more and more time working on Pencils of Promise than he did on the multi-million-dollar clients at Bain. Eventually, faced with an ultimatum, Adam had to choose between the two. His parents thoroughly encouraged him to continue his career on Wall Street after he had worked so hard to get there, but he was determined to follow his passion. "Even the people who love you most are sometimes going to disagree with you," Adam said. "But if you have that inner voice that tells you: this is why I'm here, this is what I'm meant to do, you can't turn away from it."[23]

Adam quit his job and committed full-time to Pencils of Promise. Twelve years later, they have built over 545 schools with more than 113,000 students.[24] His life looks much different today than he imagined it would when he was in school, but he is thankful that his journey led him to discover his passion. "Things happen for a reason," Adam stated. "I think every single person is here by design. You wouldn't just kind of be in the situations that you're in unless you had some higher purpose that you're meant to achieve."[25]

When true passion hits, it's almost impossible to ignore. Adam tried to return to the life he had planned for himself before his voyage, but he was so inspired by the vision to help kids go to school that he could no longer return to his former career path—he just wasn't the same. The allure and excitement of attaining a successful career on Wall Street dried up the instant he was struck with a deeper calling. Despite his efforts to connect his career to his newfound passion, it didn't work. It was too far removed. The motivation to attain wealth to help others wasn't sustaining enough compared to the overwhelming sense of fulfillment in seeing a kid's eyes light up at the gift of a pencil. He had found what truly made him come alive.

FINDING YOUR PASSION

Finding our passion in life is the starting point of our journey toward purpose. It lights up the areas in our lives we should pay close attention to that hold the potential for immense meaning. This can help us find true fulfillment in our lives. But there are different kinds of passions that don't all produce the same thing. Sometimes it simply describes our motivation or intensity, but intrinsic passion is more than that. It is a source of energy found deep within our soul that is not derived from accomplishments or contingent on the outcome of our endeavors.

Like any search, finding the things that give us energy requires us to explore the world and learn about different problems, experiences, and people. Doing so will allow us to see what ignites the most excitement within us and empower us to test the most sustainable options. If we are going to live with purpose, we need to understand how to find our true passion and how to differentiate that from the many other things that seek to motivate us in life.

If you have ever spent an extended amount of time at a beach, it's very likely that you would have seen someone walking through the sand with a metal detector trying to uncover treasure buried underground. For many, it is a fun hobby to search for lost items of value by listening to the beeping detector tell them when they are hovering over any precious metals. In the same way that device works, passion acts like a detector that helps us identify our purpose. When we get close to areas of meaning in our lives, it will alert us like an alarm as we feel a rush of energy and excitement. This sudden jolt should prompt us to pause and begin to look around for the purpose that may be nearby.

But just because the metal detector beeps doesn't mean one has struck gold. There are plenty of other metal objects that can set it off. It's impossible to know for sure what we have found until we uncover, test, and inspect it. In the same way, not all passion has the same value either. Some things we are zealous about won't lead to purpose and may even cause us to burn out. That is why it is essential to inspect the source of our passion so we can differentiate between that which is sustaining and that which is draining.

Our motivations in life fall into two distinct categories— extrinsic and intrinsic motivators. In order to understand the difference, we need to analyze the source of what is really driving us to do something. Extrinsic motivation is reward-driven, not derived from the work itself but in the result that the work produces—money, titles, status, praise. One example is the desire and motivation one could feel to work on Wall Street, not for the love of helping people but instead because of the wealth that it can provide. Another would be playing a sport in high school not because we really enjoy it, but because it will make our parents happy. These sources of motivation aren't a result of doing the work itself and don't produce sustaining passion in our lives.

Intrinsic motivation—on the other hand—is derived solely from the enjoyment found in doing an activity and nothing else. There is no additional reward needed to motivate us. If you've ever heard someone say, *"I can't believe they are paying me to do this!"* that is a sign of intrinsic motivation. We aren't driven by any result but simply by the joy found in doing the work itself. Adam discovered intrinsic motivation in helping kids get access to education. And, when he did, he realized it produced a sustaining source of passion that was stronger than anything else in his life.

In both categories of motivation, our passion can become an intense desire or enthusiasm for something that drives us forward. But for it to fulfill and sustain us, we should look for things we are intrinsically motivated to do—the energy that is found simply in the activity itself, not based on the result or reward we get from doing something. This search is salient because results or outcomes are not always in our control. When we are driven by things outside of our control, we run the risk of losing our passion if those events don't come to pass.

So, what makes you feel truly alive? For Adam, that question was only answered after his experience in India. He needed to try different things and follow his curiosity to explore what he really wanted to do with his life. He enjoyed his career and was driven to become successful enough to help others, but that motivation wasn't derived from the work itself. It paled in comparison to the passion he experienced from seeing the difference a pencil made in a child's life, which led him to find his purpose.

Finding our true passion will require some intentional thought. For most of us, life has buried the clues that would lead us there over years of financial constraints, limited time, doubts of our abilities, or indifference to begin even looking. The dreams of what we wanted to be when we grew up, which once came so effortlessly as a kid, faded away as we grew older. If we don't do anything, we can become calloused and lose the ability to entertain such thoughts. We need to give ourselves permission to dream again and overcome the enemies of passion that hinder us from finding what makes us wholeheartedly come alive.

THE ENEMIES OF PASSION

When it was time for me to pick a major in college, I chose to study engineering for two reasons—I was good at math, and engineers made a lot of money. I had learned the value of a dollar early on in life and saw the painful consequences that can occur when finances are tremendously tight. This led me to prioritize the financial potential in my career choice over the intrinsic passion found in performing the job alone. It wasn't until I actually went off to school and experienced starting a business that I found I really had a passion for helping people.

Once I discovered that passion, I thought to myself, "If I could help someone manage their money effectively, I could help them avoid many problems in life and with their family." I reasoned further that if someone would trust me with their money, they could likely trust me with other parts of their life, allowing me to help give guidance and wisdom. What better way to help people? The more I thought about it, the more excited I became—and ultimately ended up switching to a finance major to become a financial advisor. I didn't graduate with a high-paying engineering job out of college, but the intrinsic motivation I found in helping others gave me the passion that led to finding purpose in my career.

The reality of financial constraints often acts as an enemy to passion in our life. We can let money become the reason we don't follow through on the things we are passionate about or think we are passionate about something when it is really just the love of money that is driving us. A great test to determine the role money has on what we do is to ask ourselves this question: if money wasn't an object, what would I do with my life? Think about how you would spend your time if you had an endless supply of wealth in your bank account.

The influence of money isn't the only thing that can affect our decisions. Self-doubt is another enemy that can keep us from living out our passion. We can have a desire to do something but then have self-limiting beliefs that we will never be good enough to make it happen. We judge our perceived capabilities before we even take a step in that direction. Doubt can be amplified when comparing ourselves to others and thinking we don't have what it takes to do what they are doing. But what if we asked ourselves these questions: "If I could do anything in the world and knew for certain that I would be great at it, what would I do? Furthermore, if I had a guarantee that I couldn't fail, would I be doing something else right now?"

Perhaps worse than any self-limiting belief is the enemy of apathy—the lack of interest, enthusiasm, or concern for something. The polar opposite of passion is apathy, and it can settle in after we feel downright defeated by uncontrollable obstacles in life. When we stop caring about things, we lose hope in the potential for our circumstances to change or the idea that there is any real meaning to life. It's a dark place to be but doesn't have to be a permanent reality. We can overcome this feeling and regain our zeal by finding things in our life that give us an intrinsic motivation that will last, no matter what we are going through.

PASSION THAT LASTS

Most people would say they find their passion in the various things that they do—the activities they are good at or enjoy that bring them energy and excitement. But even if our passion comes from the activities themselves and not a particular reward, it is still a requirement that we do those specific activities to find fulfillment. Once we stop or can no longer do those things, the passion we get from them ceases as well. What if there was a better place to look? What if there was a place we could find passion that would go along with us wherever we went, no matter what we are doing? That would make it something internal to who we are that could never be taken away from us. Such a place does exist, and we can find it when we look for passion in living for the principles we highly value instead of the activities we take part in. When we look at our values, it will point us to purpose no matter what we do.

One group that exemplifies this is the United States Marine Corps. The values a marine possesses are honor, courage, and commitment. When they sign up to serve our country, these core values become a part of their identity and the birthplace of passion that drives them to live, fight, and sacrifice their lives for something bigger. In their words, they are the "building blocks that will aid in making the right decisions at the right time, both on the battlefield and in our Nation's communities."[26] To become a Marine is to adopt these values as a source of passion that fuels everything they do. Even long after leaving the battlefield and coming home, these principles remain a source of passion influencing everything they do in life.

What are the values you stand for? What principles bring up the most amount of passion within you? Having a set of core values that are the source of energy in life will lead us to find purpose no matter what we are doing. We need words that we esteem to live by that stir up excitement and loyalty anytime we think about them. Finding the values that make you tick will ignite your passion and allow you to find purpose regardless of your circumstances. It is no longer dependent on *what* you are doing but rather on *why* you are doing it. You can live out these values in the various roles you might already have—parent, spouse, friend, coworker, etc. In some cases, your values may lead you to pursue something different, but identifying what they are will be a part of determining your purpose as you tap into your passion.

When we are intentional in identifying the core values that drive us, it will establish the first building block of purpose in our lives. Then we can build upon them by better understanding ourselves and knowing who we are. That will require an inward journey of reflection and self-discovery that will challenge us to be authentic and own our stories, which we will explore in the next chapter.

ACTIVITY—FINDING YOUR PASSION

The following exercise is designed to help you identify your core values. The list on the next page is not all-encompassing, but it is a start toward identifying what really makes you tick.

STEP 1: CIRCLE

Read through each value listed below and circle the ones that stir something inside of you. If one comes to mind that you don't see, write it below in the space provided. Don't limit yourself on how many you circle or write down.

Core Values

Responsibility	Passion	Backbone	Fearless
Hard Work	Boldness	Honesty	Exploration
Commitment	Victory	Truth	Present
Discipline	Joy	Consistency	Productive
Selflessness	Heart	Dedication	Awareness
Leadership	Strength	Humility	Reverence
Balance	Character	Competence	Candor
Integrity	Vision	Endurance	Growth
Mental Strength	Courage	Decisiveness	Harmony
Love	Respect	Confidence	Serenity
Faith	Loyalty	Purpose	Hope
Connection	Ethical	Intelligence	Thoughtful
Curiosity	Understanding	Openness	Structure
Drive	Learning	Welcoming	Meaning
Patience	Stewardship	Optimism	Service
Energy	Poise	Teamwork	Tolerance
Intensity	Generosity	Spirituality	Timeliness
Support	Sincerity	Honor	Spontaneous
Charity	Transparency	Humor	Capable
Calm	Inquisitive	Excellence	Communication
Liberty	Independence	Brave	Maturity
----------	----------	----------	----------

STEP 2: RANK

After you've made your selections, rank the values you circled from most important to least.

STEP 3: TAKE ACTION

Then, write down your top 3–5 values somewhere you will see every day as a reminder to look for ways you can express them in your relationships at work, at home, and with friends. Let these core values give you a new sense of purpose and duty to everything you do.

6

AUTHENTICITY: BE YOURSELF

———

"Owning our story and loving ourselves through that process is the bravest thing that we will ever do."

—BRENÉ BROWN

As a research professor who studied courage, vulnerability, and shame, Brené Brown was fascinated by people's stories. She was driven to learn and better understand people's experiences with these qualities in their life. After spending six years gathering research and interviews, her findings took her down a road of self-discovery she wasn't prepared for. It was a painful journey that, in the end, left her questioning her own career path.

Brené graduated from the University of Texas at Austin in 1995 with a bachelor's degree in social work. She went on to get both a master's degree and her PhD in social work at the University of Houston. When she started her doctorate program, she had to pick a topic to research. Brené decided that she would study people's connections with others because of the critical role relationships have in our lives. "By the time you're a social worker for ten years," she said, "... what you realize is that connection is why we're here. It's what gives purpose and meaning to our lives. This is what it's all about."[27]

About six weeks into her research, Brené ran into something unidentifiable that seemed to have a devastating impact on people's relationships. She stopped her interviews and studied the stories she had collected so far to see if she could pinpoint what this phenomenon was that was inhibiting people's ability to connect. "It turned out to be *shame*," she said, "... and shame is really easily understood as the fear of disconnection."[28]

Brené's one-year research quest turned into six years as her topic shifted to focus specifically on this new concept of "shame." She organized the stories she had gathered into two groups—those who had an effortless ability to connect, along with a strong sense of love and belonging, and those who really struggled with it. The main difference, she discovered, was very simply that the first group believed they were worthy of love and belonging. This development caused curiosity to arise in her both on a personal and professional level—what did the first group possess that led to this belief?

Combing through her research, she looked at all the stories in this first group for clues. She discovered three common themes they all shared—they all possessed the courage to be imperfect, had compassion toward themselves, and formed connections as a result of being authentic. She labeled this group with the first word that came to her mind as she thought about what best described them: "wholehearted."

As these themes continued to show up in her data, a thread arose that connected them all together—the people that had an easier time connecting were those who could be vulnerable. They didn't view vulnerability as something comfortable or easy, but it wasn't entirely painful either. They just simply saw it as something that was necessary. The research concluded that if shame was the culprit causing disconnection, then the willingness to be vulnerable was the antidote.

These findings completely shocked Brené. She had set out on this research journey to control and predict behaviors that fostered a connection between people—but, as it turns out, the conclusion of her research is to live with vulnerability and to stop controlling and predicting! This realization caused her to have a personal crisis. "I became a researcher to avoid vulnerability, and when being vulnerable emerged from my data as being absolutely essential to wholehearted living, I had a breakdown." This breakdown led her to see a therapist to work through her personal journey to become more wholehearted. Little did she know how this was preparing her for what was next.[29]

In 2010 at TEDxHouston, Brené gave her first TED Talk titled "The Power of Vulnerability." She shared the story of her research with about five hundred people in the audience, including the part about her personal crisis. It went so well the organization published her talk online, and within a few hours, the video had gone viral. The following day Brené recalls having "the worst vulnerability hangover of my life." She was trying to get her work out to the world yet wanted to remain under the radar, unexposed. There was a part of her that desired to stay small to avoid shame and still have a big impact.[30]

As those desires conflicted within her, she had a choice to make. She could either step forward onto this new terrifying platform in front of her or turn in the other direction and run toward what was comfortable. Brené chose to embrace her story and the vulnerability that came along with it. She mustered up the courage to accept the national attention her work suddenly received because she knew from her research that vulnerability was the path to greater clarity in her purpose.

Today, that original TED Talk has over fifty million views. Brené has authored five No. 1 New York Times Best Sellers. She has shared her work around the world as a highly sought-after speaker and most recently did a Netflix special on vulnerability titled *The Call to Courage*. "Vulnerability is hard, and it's scary, and it feels dangerous," admits Brené. "But it's not as hard, scary, or dangerous as getting to the end of our lives and having to ask ourselves—'*What if I would have shown up?*'"[31]

Brené had a story with immense purpose, and yet she almost didn't realize its potential because she was afraid of being vulnerable. When her work first entered the world stage, it amplified her fears of not being worthy enough. Faced with an important choice, she either decided to go through the pain of being vulnerable or go through the pain of denying her purpose and hiding. It wasn't easy, but by choosing to have the courage to be vulnerable, she was able to be wholly authentic and go down the path of purpose.

The stories of our lives often lead us to similar crossroads. The resulting choice we have is to either own our story by being authentic or hide who we are by pretending to be someone else. For purpose to be present and flourish in our lives, we need to have the courage to choose authenticity—to embrace our story and put to good use the gifts, talents, and abilities we already possess. Otherwise, we will become over-run with fear and driven to become someone we are not just to avoid experiencing the painful feelings of not being good enough. But scary as those fears might be, there is immense joy found on the other side as we choose to be authentic and live a fulfilling life of purpose.

KNOW YOUR STORY

The first step in becoming more authentic is to know our story. Starting the journey of self-discovery is a rewarding experience that helps us understand our personality better, along with our strengths and weaknesses. The more we know about ourselves, the more authentic we can be. It starts with asking questions that point us to look within. Some examples include: What inspires me? What scares me? What qualities and attributes make me who I am? What habits do I revert to when I face challenges? These questions turn our focus inward to better comprehend what makes us who we are. Until we can genuinely connect with all parts of ourselves, it is exceptionally challenging to be vulnerable with others and live authentically.

Sometimes our personality can actually interfere with us being our true selves. That happened to me as the detail-oriented, critical, analyzing part of my personality took over control of my social interactions and inhibited my intuition. It was only through an awareness of those tendencies that I could disarm them and become my authentic self. We often build up walls around our flaws and despised qualities out of self-preservation. Instead, if we grow our awareness through self-discovery, we can reconnect with the parts of us that are the most genuine. One tool I found extremely helpful in doing that is the Enneagram. It strips back the layers of our personality and highlights our core desires and fears. The results reveal the ways our personality can become overprotective and hide who we really are.

There are several fears that can put our personality into this overdrive mode. Fear of failure, rejection, abandonment, and unworthiness are some examples. They are scary experiences that can cause us to protect ourselves from their pain by acting differently than we naturally would. These fears can overtake our lives and cause us to manufacture different versions of ourselves to keep us from experiencing them. Our personality may have good intentions, but in its attempts to help us avoid these painful feelings, it impedes us from becoming authentic. Sacrificing who we are just to avoid failure, abandonment, unworthiness, or rejection will not lead us down the path to purpose.

These worries can be summed up as the fear of "not being good enough." That somehow, at our core, we do not possess what it takes to fit in, that we are not worthy of belonging, or that we have nothing meaningful to offer the world. That fear is experienced in our lives as shame. Shame is a crippling emotion that cuts to the heart of who we are by attaching to our identity and keeping us hidden in the shadows. It is the number one detractor to living a life of authenticity.

ENGAGE YOUR STORY

In Brené Brown's book *Daring Greatly*, she defines the concept of "shame" as "an intensely painful feeling or experience of believing that we are flawed and therefore unworthy of love and belonging." This feeling of being flawed and unworthy is what separates the experience of shame from that of guilt, humiliation, or embarrassment. Shame is the sense that, at our core, we are defective and don't measure up. In response, we often strive to earn our standing among others by hiding our imperfections and becoming the person we need to be to fit in to dispel these painful feelings.

Shame grows out of the belief that our flaws are a sign of weakness, causing us to be unworthy of acceptance. We try to hide our perceived inadequacies out of self-defense. By keeping them hidden and our shame a secret, we hope to avoid the pain that could ensue if they were to be exposed. This can manifest itself in various ways as our personality seeks to protect us. It becomes a bitter two-edged sword—get close to others by being ourselves and risk feeling shame, or distance ourselves from others and risk feeling alone. Faced with the choice between the lesser of these two evils, the threat of shame can keep us cut off from being ourselves and prevents us from stepping into purpose. But what if the very thing that has been causing shame in our lives is actually pointing us to our purpose?

Christine Caine was born in Australia in 1966—without a name. Her biological parents had abandoned her shortly after giving birth to her. Growing up with her adopted family, Christine never felt like she fit in. Her mom would criticize her for not wanting to play with dolls or join ballet, like all the other girls at school. Tragically, her experience of abuse did not stop at bullying; by the time she was fifteen, she had been sexually abused by multiple men. Christine couldn't recall a time during her childhood where she didn't feel ashamed: "When you start being abused, you think what is happening to you is wrong. I think as it continues, over a sustained period of time, you begin to think there's something wrong with you."[32]

When she turned twenty-one, something happened that gave her power over her circumstances. Faith became a new priority of hers as she devoted her life to following Jesus. She began looking to God for a new identity. The pain and feelings of shame were still present, but her journey toward healing had begun. She found her value in who God said she was instead of deriving it from the people who hurt her. Christine fought to make what Jesus did for her in dying on the cross bigger than what anyone else had done to her during her childhood. "My whole goal is to say that Jesus 'put shame to shame' on the cross. Isaiah 53 says he died for our shame."[33]

It took many years for Christine to find complete healing from all of the abuse she had experienced, but her life looks much different today. What was once an area of great shame has become a source of profound purpose. She founded the A21 Campaign, which rescues and cares for women and children who are caught up in the abuse of human trafficking. Christine eventually shared her story through books and sermons across the world. "Although a lot of bad things happened to me," she said, "… my life is a testimony that God can take the bad things that happened to you and turn them around for his glory."[34]

Christine's story is one of remarkable bravery. The painful abuse she experienced could have easily ended in despair and depression. It wasn't an easy road, but Christine found hope in God that allowed her to turn her shame into a platform to help others. Her faith empowered her to face her fears and share her painful experiences with the world by being genuine and vulnerable—a tremendous act of courage. As she took steps to be more authentic, her faith grew. She overcame the weight of her shame and started living out her purpose.

OWN YOUR STORY

The irony with shame is that it actually festers and grows the most in silence—the more we hide or ignore it, the more we feel it. Silence acts like an incubator that amplifies its voice in our lives. The answer, as Brené discovered, is not to run from our shame but to embrace it head-on—to be authentic and vulnerable instead of seeking to avoid or conceal our shame. When we own our full story by accepting who we are, along with all our perceived flaws, shame retreats. It cannot survive outside the protection of silence. Choosing to be authentic may seem scary, but if we can find the courage to be vulnerable, it will destroy shame and lead us to our purpose.

Living from a place of authenticity was something I struggled with growing up. It started in high school when I made a vow to myself to change my persona. I had just finished my middle school years and was growing increasingly insecure with the way I looked, acted, and dressed. Friends during that time would always look for opportunities to poke fun as a means of affection, but I always took it personally. I looked at high school as an opportunity for a fresh start and decided I would try to change my perception—to look my best and act in a way that would win the acceptance of others.

That vow was so ingrained in my decision-making process it became second nature to filter myself constantly. This mentality of controlling my behavior regarding socializing was exhausting. I felt like I should have eventually outgrown it, but it stayed with me long after graduating college. There was so much pressure to do and say the right thing because I was afraid of being rejected—that no one would like me. It became a habit that was hurting me way more than it was ever helping. I was so stressed out from overthinking that I felt lonely and depressed.

Thankfully, my counselor, Andy, helped point out that I had been evaluating my social interactions based on the wrong metric. I had developed this pattern of measuring success based on the outcome of my interactions—based on if I thought the other person liked me. In realizing that, I changed the manner in which I evaluated all my social interactions. Instead of the win being a specific outcome, I replaced that goal with a mindset that only focused on whether I was fully authentic. By measuring success based simply on showing up and expressing my true self, I removed my overanalyzing thoughts and honored who I genuinely was. This shift turned out to be incredibly freeing and empowering as I never realized my ultimate fears.

When we interact with others, there is always the pull to put our best foot forward. But the risk we run in doing that is the very thing we are trying to avoid: disconnection. Disclosure is the currency of intimacy, meaning the more we are open and authentic, the deeper our relationships will be with others and with ourselves. In her book *The Gifts of Imperfection*, Brené summed up the idea of "authenticity" as a series of choices: *"Authenticity is a collection of choices that we have to make every day. It's about the choice to show up and be real. The choice to be honest. The choice to let our true selves be seen."*

THE COURAGE TO BE YOURSELF

It takes a lot of courage to show up and let your authentic self be seen in the face of fear, but allowing yourself to be seen by owning your story is one of the bravest things you will ever do. We often idolize superheroes in movies who overcome the villain to save the world, but do you realize that you are the hero of your own story? You have the power to be courageous by choosing to be your authentic self in the face of fear. You have an immeasurable worth within your unique story. No one has the same talents, experiences, thoughts, and feelings as you do. It can seem overwhelming at first, but by starting with a tiny step of courage, you can get there one decision at a time.

One small step you can take today is to decide to respond authentically to the simple question we get asked all the time: "How are you?" It has become synonymous with saying "Hello" in our culture, not meant as an actual question. Some years ago, I became friends with a woman from Germany who had just moved to Chicago. She was very confused why people greeted her by asking how she was doing but then didn't expect an honest answer. We are so used to it; we think nothing of it. Often our responses are, "I'm good, how are you?" when, in reality, we are not OK but don't want to bother the other person. Or we might say, "I'm good, just a little tired," when we really have something weighing us down. It may seem small but choosing to be authentic every time you are asked that question will turn on your awareness of your level of authenticity.

You can also build your authenticity muscle and strengthen your courage by evaluating the areas of your life that hold the most amount of shame. What parts of yourself do you most often hide from others? Are there parts of your story or personality you wish were different? What causes you to shrink down in fear and keeps you from being authentic? Answering these questions with honesty will help you identify the areas in your life that will require the most courage. It doesn't mean you need to broadcast them to everyone, but by simply telling someone you really trust your honest, raw feelings, you will experience the power vulnerability has over shame. That will give you the courage to become more authentic in every area of your life.

Though, the most momentous decision to expel shame from our lives is the one to get our identity from who God says we are instead of anyone else, just as Christine did to overcome the darkest corners of her life. She believed God loved her just as she was and had a plan for her life. That empowered her to overcome all the shame from the abuse she experienced. The darkness in our lives is redeemed when we realize that we are children of God, born with immeasurable worth and an identity rooted in who He says we are. No amount of shame can stand against knowing the value and love that God has placed upon our lives. Stepping into this truth is immensely liberating. It gives us the ability to live authentically and turn our shame into a platform of purpose.

Every day we have a choice to make—to either honor our true selves and own our stories; or to hide and pretend. By deciding to acknowledge how we feel in authentic ways, we permit ourselves to live openly and genuinely. It requires a lot of courage, but in the end, it will lead us to discover the meaning our stories possess and allow us to live our lives with a profound purpose. This level of authenticity will often result in facing the pain in our lives head-on. But as we will see in the next chapter, even the pain we experience in life can lead us to new opportunities to express our purpose.

ACTIVITY—DISARMING OUR PERSONALITY: THE ENNEAGRAM

There are several different personality tests you can take to understand the unique gifts and talents that make up who you are. It is best to explore as many of those as you can. I mentioned one that was instrumental in my journey of self-discovery called the Enneagram. It breaks down our personality and helps us know ourselves more deeply by understanding the motivations behind the choices we make. It also lays out a path for personal growth. It exposes our behavior objectively by identifying the ways our personality becomes overprotective and restricts our authenticity. Below are the steps to help you begin a journey of self-discovery and live out your true self.

STEP 1: ASSESS AND REFLECT

Start by taking the online assessment below. Then read the descriptions of the top two or three numbers you ranked the highest in to determine which one best fits you. Although there are nine options total, only one will be your primary. Once that primary has been selected, it is possible that you can share qualities of the adjacent numbers on either side of your main number, called wings. If you need further clarity on which one best describes you, ask for feedback from a few close friends or family members.

Online Enneagram assessment:
https://assessment.yourenneagramcoach.com/

STEP 2: DIG DEEPER

Once you identify your number, use the link below to study it deeper to understand how your personality responds under stress and during growth. Read the "Levels of Development" section to identify your healthy and unhealthy levels so you can discern your path forward to make progress. Studying your number will increase your awareness of how your personality gets in the way of living out your true self.

Overview of each personality type:
https://www.enneagraminstitute.com/type-descriptions

STEP 3: GROW YOUR AWARENESS

Finally, sign up for a daily email that will send you a simple thought to consider each day, which can help you continue to grow and express authenticity in all your interactions.

Daily Email:
https://subscriptions.enneagraminstitute.com/subscribers/create

7

PAIN: LISTEN TO YOUR TRAUMA

"God whispers to us in our pleasures, speaks in our conscience, but shouts in our pains: it is his megaphone to rouse a deaf world."

—C.S. LEWIS

In 2013, Rebekah Gregory traveled to Boston for the weekend of her twenty-sixth birthday with her five-year-old son, Noah, and a group of friends. They started the weekend by completing a full list of activities exploring the city, including going to a Red Sox game. On that Sunday, they planned to spend the day cheering on one of their friends who was running the Boston Marathon. As soon as the race was over, they were going to head back home to Houston. But the tragic events that unfolded before they left changed the course of Rebekah's life forever.

Massive crowds lined both sides of the street, cheering and clapping as the runners flew by. Rebekah and her friends made their way to the seventeenth-mile marker, but Noah was growing increasingly bored from hopping around to different places, so Rebekah took him and split from their friends. They jumped ahead to the finish line so they could rest while they waited for everyone else to catch up. Rebekah found the perfect spot to watch the end of the race, and because Noah was exhausted, he sat down in front of his mother's feet, with his back resting up against her shins. They were content there as they waited for Rebekah's friend to finish the race.

Suddenly, a bomb exploded three feet behind them, which thrust Rebekah into the air and slammed her down, pinning her to the ground. She tried to move but could only lift her head to look around. Her legs were so badly mangled they were unrecognizable. There was debris and blood everywhere that made it look like a scene from a horror movie. All she could think about was her son. Hearing his screams, she realized Noah was right behind her, terrified from the blast—but he seemed to be okay. Her body had acted as a human shield that protected him, leaving him with only a deep cut on his shin.

Rebekah, on the other hand, was in critical condition. She was rushed to the hospital and put into a medically-induced coma as they began emergency surgery. That coma lasted for a week, followed by surgery after surgery to repair the injuries all over her body. She was in the hospital for almost two months and underwent a total of sixty surgeries. She lost over seventy-nine pounds during that time with internal damage so severe that she was told she could never have kids again. The doctors worked extremely hard to save her left leg, which had taken the brunt of the trauma—but, after seventeen more surgeries over the course of a year, they decided it was time to amputate it.

Living life as an amputee was not something Rebekah ever thought would be a reality for her, but losing her leg became a welcome ending to the battle of never-ending pain. She wrote a breakup letter to her leg (as if it were a bad boyfriend) that reflected her comedic spirit along her road to recovery. As her physical wounds healed, she continued to suffer from the posttraumatic stress of the bombing. Rebekah credits her faith in God as the source of strength that helped her make it through her darkest days. "There are some days where it's awful, and I'm like, 'Why did I survive? Why do I have to do this?'" Rebekah said. "But for every one of those bad days, God is there. And if I didn't have faith in a bigger plan and faith that he is more powerful than all of my problems put together, what would I have? What would be the motivation to get up every day if there is nothing to get up for?"[35]

It would have been easy for Rebekah to just give up—to become overwhelmed by what happened to her and the sad reality that life as she knew it would never be the same. But instead, she found purpose in her pain and courage to stand up against the terrorist who carried out the attack. In an open letter to the bomber, Rebekah declared her determination to use the pain inflicted on her life for something bigger. "What you tried to destroy, you only made stronger," she said, "because now you have given me (and the other survivors) a tremendous platform to help others and essentially do our parts in changing the world for the better."[36]

Months after the surgery, Rebekah received a prosthetic leg and decided to start training to run the Boston Marathon.

It was no simple task, but she was determined to use this goal to symbolize the rise out of her pain to take her life back. Every day, she worked on getting physically stronger through training and therapy. She quickly progressed from relying on a wheelchair to learning to balance, walk, and eventually run. During the 2015 Boston Marathon later that year, Rebekah ran the last 3.2 miles of the race to cross the finish line in the exact same place her life was forever changed just two years earlier. It was a tremendous accomplishment and a symbol of her resilient spirit that would not let her life be defined by what happened.[37]

The painful, terrifying events that turned her life upside down became an enormous opportunity to inspire others. Rebekah later wrote a book titled *Taking Back My Life* that retold her journey and shared a message of hope for those facing similar life-changing obstacles. She started a foundation called Rebekah's Angels to raise money to aid in the treatment of childhood trauma and PTSD as she experienced how hard it was to get help for Noah. And, in 2020, Rebekah started a podcast called *From Pain to Purpose*, where she began interviewing other people who have found meaning and purpose out of the unavoidable pain in their lives to spread a message of hope. "I truly believe that I've found my purpose in life, and it's to inspire and encourage other people," she said. "If my words can do something like that for someone, I would get blown up again tomorrow."[38]

Rebekah suffered a devastating, life-altering injury that was entirely out of her control. It was of no fault of her own she was standing where she was when the bombs went off. She could have easily fallen into depression and despair as she was helpless to the immense amount of agony the attack caused, but instead, it had a different outcome in her life. Most people look at pain as a wholly negative thing. They view suffering as something that should be avoided at all costs. But Rebekah saw things differently and eventually declared she would willingly go through her experience all over again. What we can learn from her story will drastically change the impact trauma and affliction can have on our lives.

THE AVOIDANCE OF PAIN

It's no secret that our lives can change in an instant. Things can be going fine one day, and then something could happen, which causes everything to spiral into a tailspin and crash to the ground. The hardest events to reconcile are the ones that are completely out of our control. We have done everything right in life yet are still visited by devastating loss. Why do bad things happen to good people? That is one of the toughest questions we face in life and can leave us questioning all that we believe. But, what if we do have a say in the matter—not in avoiding things from happening, but in choosing how we respond to them?

We learn from a young age that pain is bad. Whenever we would do something wrong, our parents would punish us by some form of discomfort—usually by being put in a time-out, getting spanked, or being grounded. Some of our actions would have a natural consequence that didn't require our parents to intervene at all—getting suspended, arrested, or fired. Parenting has long incorporated punishments to teach their kids how to behave because it has a powerful ability to mold our behavior.

But when it comes to our personal growth and finding purpose, is avoiding pain the answer? What once served us and our parents as kids might no longer serve us as we mature into adulthood. In fact, what if going through pain actually produced growth in our lives in a way that nothing else ever could?

Rebekah didn't choose to get blown up that day in Boston. But she did choose how she responded to the pain and trauma that followed in her life. She didn't run or hide from it but sought help from both physical and mental experts to work with her through the post-traumatic stress she experienced. After months of seeing a counselor and leaning into her faith, Rebekah was well on her way to healing. She admits there are still hard days, but her outlook on what happened has changed entirely. She now sees the platform to help others that this painful event gave her instead of all the things it took away.

THE PURPOSE IN PAIN

Millions of Americans work out every day at health clubs across the country; they seek to put their body under a certain amount of physical stress to stay in shape. Our muscles are designed in such a way that in order for them to grow, they need to experience micro-tears that turn on the body's healing mechanism. They need to be broken down so they can regrow stronger. There is no shortcut to increasing physical strength without enduring the pain and soreness in our muscles caused by working out.

Sometimes in the pursuit of growing stronger, we push it too hard and suffer an unexpected injury. We might sprain our ankle, pull a muscle, or break a bone, derailing our ability to function normally. If we think we've broken something, our natural response is to go to the doctor to get an X-ray. We don't even second guess it when our foot is swelling up and changing colors. It is clear we cannot fix this on our own; we need the care of a medical expert to help our body heal properly. However, when it comes to emotional injuries, we don't see them in the same light. There is often a stigma associated with seeing a psychologist. Even though something might break mentally, we don't take the time to get it checked out or seek expert help to begin the process of healing.

In the same way that a broken foot needs a cast to heal properly, our mind needs help processing our suffering in order to heal correctly. But instead of listening to that pain, we often think we can make it go away by ignoring it or developing our own coping habits. Some of these habits can be a naturally healthy response, while others are completely destructive and prevent us from getting better. We can't just change our attitude, turn to drugs, or distract ourselves and expect our emotional distress to just disappear. Instead, we need to lean into the discomfort by listening to our pain and getting expert help. That will allow us to go through the necessary process of grieving to heal adequately.

Grieving is the psychological-emotional experience we have following the loss of any kind; as we think about what we lost and how life may never be the same, uncomfortable feelings set in. It could be from the loss of a job, relationships, loved one, physical ability—any occurrence of a loss in our life. According to the Kübler-Ross model, we go through five stages of grief on the path to healing: denial, anger, bargaining, depression, and acceptance. It is easy to get stuck in denial and anger without fully processing our feelings to get to a place of acceptance. When we avoid dealing with a loss of any kind, it prevents us from not only fully healing but also from creating the capacity for something greater to grow.

In 2009, Ashley Jones gave birth to her beautiful, healthy daughter Skylar. She and her husband were both filled with joy at the sight of this delightful new addition to their family. They brought her home and treasured her presence. But two months later, tragedy struck. Skylar was diagnosed with Spinal Muscular Atrophy, a disease similar to ALS (Amyotrophic Lateral Sclerosis) that attacks the body's muscles, destroying their ability to function correctly. Shortly after the diagnosis, Skylar lost her ability to swallow and required her first surgery.[39]

Ashley and her husband were heartbroken. The prognosis was that Skylar wouldn't make it a full year. Afraid that she might not survive the first procedure, they asked one of their close friends, who was a photographer, to come and take pictures of Skylar so they could capture and hold on to the memories of her forever. Skylar came out of the first surgery successfully, and Ashley's friends gifted them a professional photography session to capture more beautiful moments with their daughter as they celebrated together.

Skylar ended up living for twenty-one months, which was a miracle, given her diagnosis. Saying goodbye was one of the hardest things Ashley had to do. Amid her grieving process, she looked through all the photos they had taken of Skylar since she was born. Revisiting these beloved memories gave her the comfort and space that helped her mourn. The pictures allowed her to feel close to her daughter as she worked through her sorrow toward letting go.

As Ashley walked through the pain and sadness, she saw a door of purpose opening in her life. She realized the power these pictures had in helping her grieve and offered to take photographs for others she knew who were facing a terminal diagnosis of any kind. She willingly stepped into the pain of her friends to help them in their own grieving process, knowing firsthand what they were going through. Ashley expanded it further and founded a nonprofit called Love Not Lost that donates portrait sessions and photo albums to families facing a terminal illness. "It is truly an honor to come alongside of people who know their time is short to capture and preserve their memory for those who love them," Ashley said. "I can't think of anything else in life for which I am more qualified."[40]

The tragedy Ashley experienced in losing her daughter was agonizing, but it created a unique opportunity for purpose in her life. The pain she carried from her devastating loss spoke to her in a way that nothing else could have and enabled her to help others facing similar circumstances. Ashley grew empathy for people walking through tragic illnesses and saw how her experience uniquely equipped her to be a blessing to them. Listening to her pain as she grieved her loss allowed the seeds of purpose to grow in her life.

THE MINDSETS TOWARD PAIN

We often do not have control over the physical and emotional afflictions we experience during our lives. They can happen suddenly, and there is nothing we can do to change the past. But we always have a choice in how we respond to the pain. We have a say in the meaning we assign it in our lives. The factor determining if we see purpose or stay stuck in anguish is the mindset we have toward the unavoidable suffering in our lives.

There are two mindsets we can have: either that of a victim mentality or that of a victor. A victim mentality is the belief that bad things always happen to us. It accepts negative experiences as just our lot in life and that there is nothing we can do about it, which causes us to fall utterly helpless over the effect the pain has on us. We grow in self-pity and turn to things that will ease our misery since its presence is here to stay. With no end in sight, we can get pulled down into a cycle of despair as we recount all that we have lost—which will never be the same.

The alternative mindset is one of a victor—the belief that you possess the capacity to overcome the worst of circumstances by choosing how you define their meaning in your life. You have the final say over how you will respond to the unavoidable sufferings you face. It is not viewed as a permanent condition we must be stuck in forever; we eventually look toward the light at the end of the tunnel. This mindset is not about being tougher than our hurts or strong enough to keep them from negatively affecting us; it is about recognizing the potential purpose they can lead us to as we grieve and process our feelings honestly. That will allow us to see how we can go from pain to purpose and have an impact on others.

Rebekah could have easily fallen into a victim mentality as she focused solely on the loss of her leg, haunted the rest of her life by the trauma of being blown up, and that her life would never be the same. But, instead, she saw the purpose in her pain. She leaned into her faith and looked to God, believing there was a greater meaning behind everything that happened. The event that was the very source of her suffering became the source of profound purpose. When she realized the platform it had given her to help others, she stepped into it—which led to her starting a foundation to raise money for kids facing PTSD and launching a podcast that seeks to support and encourage others.

What pain, suffering, or unique circumstances have you gone through in life? In what ways has that experience specifically equipped you to help others? We may not have faced the level of life-changing events that Rebekah did, but we have all gone through various challenges, setbacks, or heartbreaks in our life. When we look at our experiences with a different mindset by seeing the purpose they contain, we realize that going through precisely what we did has equipped us for something greater. The pain or stressful circumstances we went through can lead us to a purpose that is bigger than we could have ever imagined without it. In order to use our experiences to help others, we need to grow our capacity to love people. In the next chapter, we will explore the different types of love and how to embrace compassion, which will enable us to make a difference in the lives of others.

ACTIVITY—PAIN JOURNALING

This exercise of journaling is an integral part of learning from our life as we process any grief, anxiety, or painful events we encounter. It will help to move us closer to a place of acceptance so we can see how our experiences have uniquely equipped us for a bigger purpose. As we take the time to write out our feelings and what we have gone through, it will allow us to better understand and accept the resulting emotions.

Below are the steps to get started and guide you through journaling on your own.

STEP 1: CREATE SPACE

Set aside some time in a quiet space where you will not be distracted and allow for at least twenty minutes to write. If you enjoy writing things longhand, then get a pad of paper and pen or, if you prefer typing, open a blank Word document. Eliminate any potential distractions and take a few deep breaths to center yourself in the moment. Let the to-do lists fade away, and just focus on what you are feeling right now.

STEP 2: IDENTIFY PROMPTS

Pick at least three questions from the list below that most resonate with you to answer. If there is a particular event or experience that you need help processing, think about that as you write. If you are not sure, then just connect with how you are feeling right now. The following journal prompts, adapted from Dr. Matthew Tull, will help kick-start your writing:

- How are you feeling right now? List any of the primary emotions you are feeling and explain why you feel that way—Sad, Angry, Scared, Happy, Excited, Tender.
- If there was a specific event that brought about these feelings, what happened? Write out the events that took place as if you were writing a book.
- What other people were involved, and how were they impacted? How did they act, and how did it make you feel?
- Explain what is causing stress in your life currently. Has this changed since your traumatic experience? If so, how? Is there a reason why that happened you can identify?

- What are you grateful for as you think through these events in your mind?
- If you could do it all over again, would you do anything differently? Why?
- Write in detail about what this experience has taught you, whether it is good or bad. What is your biggest takeaway? How is this affecting you now?
- Thinking deeper, in what ways might you be able to use this experience to help others?

STEP 3: WRITE FREELY

Start writing whatever comes to mind for as long as you can. Don't edit or reread what you are writing; just let the words flow from your thoughts onto the page until you get them all out. Once you are completely done, pray for God to speak to you as you read through what you wrote.

8

COMPASSION: LOVE YOUR NEIGHBOR

———

*"Let us not love in word or talk
but in deed and in truth."*

—1 JOHN 3:18

When tragedy struck on September 11, 2001, several heroes risked their lives to help save others. Welles Crowther was one of those people. He grew up in New York, the oldest of three kids with strong family values, and deeply admired his parents. His father had this habit of bringing a red handkerchief to church with him every Sunday. Welles looked up to his dad and wanted to be just like him. When he was six, his father gave him a red handkerchief of his very own, and he was beyond delighted. He brought it everywhere. Even as he grew older, Welles never left the house without it. That red bandana became one of his signature trademarks, which would later symbolize his legacy of touching the hearts of people far into the future.

In high school, Welles spent a lot of time around the fire station since his dad worked for the local department. He would help wash the trucks, and, when he was sixteen, he joined the Empire Hook & Ladder Company No. 1 Fire Department as a junior member. Then, at eighteen, Welles completed the state training to become a full member of the volunteer fire squad. He played lacrosse during high school and later went on to play for Boston College. Everyone knew him for his team spirit and compassion as an active member of the Fellowship of Christian Athletes.

After graduating with a degree in economics, Welles went to work for Sandler O'Neill + Partners, an investment banking firm on the 104th floor of the World Trade Center in New York City. Even in his professional career, he had a reputation for always having a red bandana with him tucked in his suit coat as he would go to the office each day. Working on Wall Street was his dream job, but after a couple of years, his heart changed. When he was twenty-four, he made the decision to switch careers to become a full-time firefighter—but before he could do that, tragedy struck.

On the morning of September 11, Welles showed up for work at 9:00 a.m. Shortly after arriving, an airplane crashed into his building about twenty floors below his office, causing a massive explosion. He called his mom within minutes and left her a voicemail, "Mom, this is Welles. I wanted you to know that I'm okay." After hanging up, he made his way down to the seventy-eighth-floor sky lobby, where he found a group of survivors among the wreckage that was in shock and very disoriented. He picked up a young woman who was severely injured and carried her on his back while telling several others to follow him as he made his way to the stairwell and down seventeen floors to working elevators.[41]

Instead of staying with them to evacuate the building, Welles returned up the stairs to help others make their way down. The smoke had gotten so bad at this point he took out his handkerchief and tied it around his mouth and nose so he could breathe. Upon returning, Welles found another group of injured people and used his firefighter training from high school to apply first aid. He told them, "Everyone who can stand, stand now. If you can help others, do so." And then he led them down the only passable stairwell, down to the working elevators.[42]

Welles made about three trips up and down those stairs before the building completely collapsed. Six months later, rescue workers found his body surrounded by firefighters and lying next to a tool called the "jaws of life," which is used to free people trapped in cars. He kept going back for more survivors until his final moment, saving eighteen people before dying. It took months for his heroic story to emerge from different survivors, but after several people reported being helped by a man in a red bandana, Welles's mom knew it was him. She connected with those survivors showing them a picture to confirm it was him, and listened to their stories.

"It's all right here in this red bandana for me," Welles's father said. "A symbol of absolutely the most pure form of compassion and love."[43] The instinct Welles had to turn back and run up those stairs into harm's way to help more people has left a historic legacy. His actions continue to inspire those he rescued to this day; as one survivor, Judy Wein, told CNN, "People can live one hundred years and not have the compassion, [or] the wherewithal to do what he did."

In 2006, Welles was posthumously named an honorary New York City firefighter. His parents created the Red Bandana Project in his honor, a character development program for classrooms, camps, and youth programs. During the dedication of the 9/11 Memorial, President Obama referred to his story in his speech, "He called for fire extinguishers to fight back the flames. He tended to the wounded. He led those survivors down the stairs to safety ... until that moment when the tower fell. They didn't know where he came from. But they knew their lives had been saved by the man in the red bandana."[44]

Welles's story proves that the most extraordinary form of love is not demonstrated in our feelings—it's shown through sacrifice. We see evidence of that in the way his actions had a lasting impact on people's lives many years later. Welles served others in their most crucial time of need by putting their well-being before his own. He exemplified a deeper kind of love that wasn't based on emotion. Through his courageous actions, he willingly risked his life in order to help people he didn't even know. We can find purpose when we embrace this kind of love that elevates the needs of others, often above our own. That is our deepest calling and humanity's greatest charge: to love your neighbor as yourself. Exhibiting this kind of love that recognizes the needs of others will allow us to see the purpose within the relationships we have. As we identify opportunities to express such selfless acts of love, it will enable us to have a profound impact on the lives of others.

REDEFINING LOVE

What comes to mind when you think of the word "love?" For many people, Hollywood's version of love has become the standard definition. Based on deeply compelling emotions that erupt between two people's affection for one another, we have elevated romantic attachment to the highest level. Our culture is obsessed with a good love story. Countless TV shows and movies portray these fairy tale stories as the pinnacle of love. Every year they make new movies depicting this kind of affection, with some of the most popular ones becoming well-known classics—films like *Titanic*, *The Notebook*, or *A Walk to Remember*. They all portray love as a strong emotion of affection between two people, leaving a story like Welles's one of the last things to come to mind.

This portrayal of love as a confluence of overpowering feelings has contributed to its excessive use in our vocabulary to describe how we feel toward many things. We can love our jobs, love this show, love this place, love that movie, love that joke, fall in love, find love at first sight, and on and on. The use of the word "love" has become so commonly used in our conversations that it is easy to misunderstand its true meaning. It has gotten watered down with its overuse in describing all the things we really like, along with our sentiment for people we really care about. But what is the true meaning of the word "love?"

According to Dr. Neel Burton, the ancient Greeks actually had seven different words to describe the concept of love. Storge (natural affection), Philia (friendship), Eros (sexual love), Agapē (unconditional love), Ludus (flirting), Pragma (committed, married love), and Philautia (self-love). Each of these words for love has a very different meaning. They differ in the magnitude and the target of love. It makes it easy to see how confusing it can be when we only use one word to describe them all. It becomes impossible to know what kind of love we are referring to without adding context. Not all of these types of love naturally lead us to express purpose in the here and now. But there is one that has the power to bring meaning into our lives, no matter where we find ourselves: the unconditional Agapē love.

Each kind of love has its place in our lives, but when it comes to impacting others, the most vital type is Agapē love (or selfless, unconditional love). That is the type of love that Welles displayed that fateful day as he risked his life in the service of others he barely knew. This love isn't based on how we are feeling or what we are getting in return. It is not confined to only those we know well or those we like. It is a radical type of love that has the power to change people's lives and the world for the better. Unconditional love will naturally create purpose in our lives once we have a heart that possesses it. To get there, we need to explore three critical components that produce this type of selfless love.

UNCONDITIONAL LOVE

The first component that is critical to have unconditional love is empathy, the ability to understand and share the feelings of another. It is a part of our emotional intelligence radar that allows us to tap into the concerns, worries, and experiences of someone else as if they were our own. It's easy for us to feel the things we have gone through in life, but when we can feel for other people's experiences, that is empathy. One of the key pieces of empathy is the ability to truly listen, see, and understand what someone is going through. If we are focused on ourselves or distracted, it is impossible to have empathy and express unconditional love. Shared experiences of suffering can be a powerful source of empathy. When we have actually gone through something others are currently facing, we are able to empathize with them since we know what it's like. But how do we have empathy for things we have never experienced?

In order for empathy to be loving, we don't actually need to go through the exact same things as someone else. We simply need to genuinely imagine what it would be like for us to do so. We need to listen to someone's pain and struggles as if they were our own. We have to cultivate a deep awareness of the other person's perspective and imagine what it would be like to be them. This process is drastically different than having sympathy for someone—which often amounts to merely feeling pity and sorrow for their misfortune. What that lacks is crossing over to experience someone's feelings with them. Sympathy allows us to stay at an arm's length away and feel bad for them, while empathy goes further to step into their shoes.

But empathy alone doesn't make us a loving person—it's merely the first step. After we share in the feelings of someone else by seeking to understand their pain, we must embrace generosity to have the willingness to give of our time, talents, or treasure to show our love for them. It could be making time to be there to listen and comfort them or by providing physical care to help ease their suffering in some way. Generosity enables us to have a level of selflessness that freely gives our resources to meet the needs of others. All the empathy in the world will not make a difference if our love remains locked behind the doors of stinginess and selfishness. When we embrace generosity, it releases our compassion into the world.

As we think about giving something to care for others, it can be easy to be protective of what we've acquired until our needs, or the needs of our family, are sufficiently met. We have a responsibility to provide for those entrusted to us and can keep all our resources directed there instead. The thought of giving to others before we have accomplished what we want can feel like we are losing something. It doesn't just apply to financial means, but to our time and talents as well. However, generosity is not a zero-sum game. There isn't only one person who wins—we can both gain something at the same time. In fact, those who have tested the waters of generosity know that giving produces greater fulfillment than keeping everything for ourselves.

After we grow in our empathy and generosity, there is one final component needed to give us the capacity to love unconditionally: compassion. Compassion is acting upon the recognized suffering of others. It represents the most significant contrast between the love displayed in romantic movies and the type of love that Welles embodied. Selfless Agapē love is defined in actions, not feelings. The difference lies in a simple choice: the decision to do something for someone in need out of the compassion we have for them. It's not always an easy decision to make because there is usually some sacrifice required—something we give up or risk losing in choosing to act. But with such actions, we will feel the true fulfillment of purpose as we step out of our comfort zones to serve the needs of others lovingly.

LOVE IN ACTION

In 1952, during the middle of the Korean War, Rev. Everett Swanson left his home in Chicago and headed off to South Korea on a mission to become a full-time evangelist. He wanted to minister to the troops that were fighting in the war. But what he thought would be a straightforward mission to share Christianity with the soldiers fighting there ended up becoming a mission to help those who were fighting a vastly different battle: poverty.

Everett arrived in Seoul and went on daily walks to familiarize himself with this city that was so new to him. He quickly discovered the devastating effects the war was having on the local families. He saw orphaned children hiding in makeshift shelters on the street huddled together to keep warm. During one of his walks, Everett noticed the local city workers scooping up piles of rags from a street corner. But as he got closer to observe what they were doing, he discovered that it wasn't rags they were scooping up—it was bodies of orphans who had died on the street the night before. The horrific sight broke his heart.

On his return trip back home, Everett could not get the images of those kids out of his mind. The extreme level of poverty he witnessed utterly devastated him. A question posed by one of his colleagues kept ringing in his ear: *"What are you going to do about the children?"*[45] As he kept thinking about that question, it moved him with compassion to do something for these kids. He knew he could not turn his back on them. Everett raised money to support a local Korean orphanage and shared the story of what he witnessed in Seoul with people he knew. Shortly after that, he had an idea to connect people's donations with a specific child, so they could sponsor them directly to provide ongoing support. This led to the birth of the organization Compassion International, which today has over 1.9 million children in its sponsorship program.[46]

Everett did not just have empathy for these kids, nor was he just generous in giving them money—he was moved with compassion to make a meaningful difference in their lives. He took action to love them by gathering resources to help them. This decision created a movement that inspired other people to join in on expressing their compassion through their actions as well. His act of love for these kids through the organization he started was a natural response from his personal experience of being loved unconditionally. Having received such love through his faith empowered him with the capacity to love others in the same way.

When someone performs a random act of kindness toward us, it often produces a desire to pay it forward as we look for ways we can do the same for someone else. Receiving this seemingly undeserved love compels us to love others. For Everett, he experienced that feeling through his faith in what God did for him despite doing nothing to deserve it. He had turned his back on God by not living up to the holy standard he was created for, just like we have all done. Yet despite our sinful behavior, God did something remarkable to pay for the penalty of our actions. Instead of the punishment of death we each deserved, he spared our life by sending his own son to die in our place. As the Bible states in Romans 5:7-8, "Very rarely will anyone die for a righteous person, though for a good person someone might possibly dare to die. But God demonstrates his own love for us in this: While we were still sinners, Christ died for us."

We have all messed up and fallen short in various areas of our lives. What we deserve as a result is punishment, but what we get instead is love. God offers us an open invitation to accept this remarkable gift of forgiveness to cleanse us from all our wrongdoings and begin a relationship with him. If you have never prayed to receive that compassion, today would be a great day to do so. When we accept such an act of love through faith, it naturally compels us to love others in a way we could not do on our own. This remarkable gift wipes away our past mistakes and inspires us to pay it forward by looking for ways to express unconditional love through our relationships.

Who in our lives right now needs our empathy, generosity, and compassion? How can we best show up in their lives to express a courageous act of selfless love to meet a need that they have? As we ask these questions more consistently and increase our awareness of the needs around us, we will strengthen this cardinal building block to purpose. There is immense potential to love others that is found in paying attention to those we encounter along our journey—family, friends, co-workers, strangers. We have opportunities to impact someone's life just because our paths happened to cross. Our awareness will increase as we let go of loving people only on our terms and begin to truly listen to the needs of others.

Let's put our love into action by identifying someone we know and committing to do one act of unconditional love for them as soon as we can. Look at the last three people on your phone that you called or texted. What is one thing you can do to express compassion toward them this week? It could be as simple as taking them out to lunch, writing them a note of appreciation, or covering some of their responsibilities so they can take a break.

Growing in our capacity to love others will lead us to find purpose within our lives, which we might never have seen before. It holds the ability to transform our relationships and profoundly impact those we meet in life. As we grow in our ability to love others more selflessly, it may feel scary. We don't know if our actions will be worth the risk or if we will get hurt somehow along the way. But if you decide not to act, then who will? Embracing these unique opportunities that show up in our lives, as we will explore next, is the final building block that will identify our calling to live with purpose.

ACTIVITY—LEARNING THE LANGUAGES OF LOVE

This exercise will help us better understand one another and get our intentions across by focusing on speaking each other's love language. According to the book *The Five Love Languages* by Dr. Gary Chapman, there are five different categories for how people communicate love. As we seek to demonstrate our compassion to others, let us learn their language so we can express our love clearly and effectively.

STEP 1: STUDY THE LANGUAGES

Read through the summary of the love languages listed below and think about examples of each one that you have experienced in your own life.

1. **Words of Affirmation:** This is demonstrated with our words—whether written or spoken through encouragement, affirmation, affection, praise, compliments, etc.

This comprises any verbal medium in which we express love and compassion.

2. **Quality Time:** This is demonstrated by spending our most precious commodity with someone: our time. But it's not just about expending time superficially; it encompasses genuinely being present and giving our undivided attention—no distractions, solely focused on them.

3. **Receiving Gifts:** This is demonstrated by physical tokens of appreciation that express our compassion or meet their physical needs. It could be a gift that is really helpful for them or very thoughtful.

4. **Acts of Service:** This is demonstrated in doing things to serve someone. Such as going out of our way to complete tasks, chores, or help with responsibilities as thoughtful demonstrations of compassion.

5. **Physical Touch:** This is expressed through an embrace. A hug, kiss, pat on the back, holding hands, or physical proximity to someone, which makes them feel that they are loved.

STEP 2: FIND YOUR LANGUAGE

Think through each category and decide which one or two resonate with you the most. Which one makes you feel the most loved? Is there one that doesn't matter to you at all? If you are unsure or want to dig deeper, follow this link to take a quiz to identify your love language: https://www.5lovelanguages.com/quizzes/.

STEP 3: LEARN THEIR LANGUAGE

Finally, read through the list again and think about the person you identified earlier, either one of the last three people you called/texted or someone you know well. Try to determine which language will best convey love to them. If you are unsure, share the list or quiz with them and ask them to pick their top one. Then speak their love language in your commitment to demonstrate your compassion toward them this week.

9

OPPORTUNITIES: FIND YOUR CALLING

———

"Heroes are made by the paths they choose,
not the powers they are graced with."

—BRODI ASHTON

Scott Neeson grew up in Australia and dropped out of school at the age of seventeen. It was hard for him to find employment without a high school degree; but after some time, he managed to get a job through a government program, working for a movie theater. Scott began overseeing the projector at night and helping as an assistant in the marketing office during the day. Slowly, his hard work gave way to more responsibility as he became a film promoter and film buyer. Eventually, in 1986, Scott became the managing director of distribution at Twentieth Century Fox Australia. With the successful trajectory that his career path was on, he would soon face a tough decision to maintain all that he had accomplished or walk away for something greater.

In 1993, Scott moved to Los Angeles to be at the heart of the Hollywood movie industry. Eventually, he became the president of Twentieth Century Fox International, managing a film budget of over a billion dollars a year for movies such as *Braveheart, Titanic, Star Wars*, and *X-Men*. For being a high school dropout, Scott had really come a long way—boasting an annual salary of over a million dollars. In 2004, he accepted a new role at Sony Pictures and negotiated a six-week vacation to take some time for himself in between changing jobs.[47]

One of the stops on his trip was in Phnom Penh, Cambodia, in Southeast Asia. After spending a couple of days exploring the city, he noticed the enormous number of children living on the streets. They would come up to him asking for money or food. It was the first time he had seen poverty like that up close. One day Scott stopped at a local café and talked to a man about the children in the community. He learned that there was a group of destitute children living close by in a place called Stung Meanchey.

Out of curiosity, he decided to visit the area the man mentioned. Scott caught a ride over and, upon arriving, was immediately in shock at what he witnessed. It turns out Stung Meanchey was a massive eighteen-acre landfill where they dumped all the garbage from the area. The heat was smoldering hot, making the fumes from the toxic trash unbearable. But the shocking part was, among the mountains of garbage, there were kids everywhere living and working in it. More than 1,500 of them were searching through the filth for plastic and metal recyclables they could sell for money. If they were lucky, they'd make only twenty-five cents a day. Some kids were left there unwanted by their parents, while others were sent there to help their family put food on the table.

"The moment I stepped on [the landfill] was the single most impactful moment in my life," Scott said.[48] He approached one of the kids, who was covered in filth and layered with clothes to protect her from the heat. Her name was Sreyoun, and she was nine years old. Scott talked with her and asked if she could take him to meet her mother. She led Scott back to her family, and he told them he was going to do something to help. He paid for them to move into a rental home and gave them enough money to eat and for Sreyoun to go to school. The total cost ended up only being thirty-five dollars a month.[49]

After returning home to his new job at Sony Pictures, he was no longer the same person. His heart was still with the kids in Cambodia and, for the next year, he traveled back once a month to Stung Meanchey to set up a charity near the garbage dump. But the stark difference between the two worlds he was living in weighed heavily on him. "You're earning more money than you ever thought possible," he said, "... living what many people consider the dream ... but the more things I acquired, from cars to houses to boats, the more I felt it was sort of a lie."[50]

The final straw came in 2004, while he was helping three kids sick with typhoid in Cambodia, and received a call from one of his actors. They yelled at Scott because their private jet had not been stocked up with their favorite amenities, telling him word for word, "My life wasn't meant to be that difficult."[51] The problems Scott was asked to solve in his Hollywood position versus the ones in Cambodia that had a life-or-death impact left him feeling significantly overwhelmed. Shortly after that, he resigned from his lucrative career and went all in to help these kids. He sold his house, his Porsche, and his yacht and moved across the world to work full-time as the founder and executive director of the Cambodian Children's Fund.

Over fifteen years later, Scott still lives in Cambodia, helping kids there get out of poverty. Sreyoun, the little girl he first met when he arrived at Stung Meanchey, has now graduated college with a degree in finance and economics. Scott has helped over 3,300 students get out of poverty through his organization.[52] Reflecting on all his work, he recalls what went through his mind during his first visit there that led him to accept this new calling: "You sort of come face to face with your own values at some point, where you can walk away or do something about it."[53] The choice he made to accept the purpose placed in front of him will impact that community for generations to come.

Scott came to a defining intersection of two paths in his life—the road of happiness through an incredibly successful career in Hollywood and the road of purpose through the streets of Cambodia. This unique opportunity hit him very unexpectedly, but it presented him with a choice he could not turn away from. Ultimately, Scott accepted the new call of purpose that came before him and cashed in all the success he achieved in his career. It was not an easy decision and took several months to make, but he could not walk away from the compassion he felt to help these children. He grew less interested in his comfortable career and became increasingly passionate about the opportunity to positively impact the lives of others.

We may soon face a similar crossroads. After living in a world that constantly points us to commit ourselves toward the pursuit of happiness, we now have identified the building blocks in our lives, which will guide us to an alternative path. The journey forward can look drastically different for everyone. We each have unique opportunities that will be specific to our lives and experiences. The temptation might be to get discouraged when we hear of people like Scott doing something so radical. We might think that we must follow in their footsteps—sell all we have and move to a developing country to find purpose—but that is not the case. There is no one-size-fits-all way to live out purpose. Instead, we must simply start looking for this final block: the opportunities to express our calling that are specific to our lives. Scott did not go to Cambodia with the goal of starting a nonprofit; the opportunity came from him just living his life. But he listened and answered the call when it arose. Just like Scott, we must pay attention to the opportunities in our lives so that we can accept the purpose they point to.

ACCEPTING THE CALL OF PURPOSE

The beautiful thing about living with purpose is it does not require us to change jobs or move to another country. It is not something we need to wait until we graduate school to do or have to be married first before we can start living purposefully. There are unique opportunities already built into our lives that will allow us to live out our purpose now. In order to have the awareness to identify them, we must change the lens through which we see our relationships, our past, our career, our identity, and our future. As we begin to look at these parts of our lives with a new perspective and intention, we will begin to see our unique opportunities. The direction we walk in life is determined by where we look; choosing to see with this new vision will allow us to recognize the meaningful opportunities already present within our lives.

Being born in the eighties, I grew up in a world where not everyone had a computer, tablet, or smartphone. Instead, we were left with old-fashioned toys that were very non-digital. But there were still some fascinating technologies of the day that were wildly popular. One of them was a book called *Magic Eye*. It was a simple paperback book with printed, repeating patterns of various colors on each page. If you looked at the design the right way, you would see an optical illusion suddenly appear. It was a three-dimensional object that floated off the page. The fun part, however, was watching other people stare at the picture for hours and not see anything different than the two-dimension random pattern of colors. Unless you knew the trick for where to focus and how to let your eyes see the hidden object, you would miss out completely.

The same thing is true for the opportunities in our life. We must know how to look for them, so we don't miss out. Accepting the call of purpose starts with deciding to view our life with a new perspective and an intention to find our calling. We must slow down and explore the places and people in need around us as we grow in the habit of looking for our opportunities. We can direct our focus based on the questions we ask ourselves throughout the day and during life's big decisions. By changing from asking "What will make me the happiest" to "What will have the biggest impact," we will start to see things differently. This awareness will help us find the unique options we have to make a difference in the world. We will then see how each of the building blocks in our life can be arranged to capitalize on the opportunities available to us. Doing so will reveal the cost of choosing this new path as we give up focusing on things that appear to maximize our enjoyment.

The old saying that "There is no free lunch" still rings true today. Accepting this new vision isn't enough to bring about change; we also need to bear the cost that accompanies choosing to pursue our unique opportunities. That doesn't mean we are destined to be unhappy the rest of our lives—quite the opposite. Happiness is one of the many byproducts of choosing to live with purpose. But we need to accept the fact that we may have to sacrifice something in the short term so that we can enjoy something far more fulfilling in the long run. Scott did that as he traded in his material success in life for significance. He sold his house, cars, and boat for the opportunity to help rescue kids in Cambodia. His friends may have thought he was crazy, but deep down, what they really knew was that he was serious. When someone is willing to make the necessary sacrifices to pursue their purpose, that is when you know they are serious.

But, being serious does not mean we have to have it all figured out first. Scott did not have everything figured out when he moved to Cambodia, other than him knowing he had a burning desire to help get kids out of poverty. The rest of his story evolved as he followed his first decision with others like it. We, too, must learn to accept the messiness that comes with not having it all figured out as we move forward into our calling. The blocks of purpose we just explored are not the equivalent of a get-rich-quick scheme. It is not a fancy new diet that will promise to help you lose ten pounds in five days—it is a lifestyle. It is simply a different way to look at our world and the life we live that, over time, will lead us down the path of purpose.

Seeing the drastic decisions that Scott and others have made in their life can be overwhelming for us to comprehend. To do what he did might require us to give up a lot of things that, frankly, we might not be ready to do yet—or ever. That is okay. Our purpose is not something we enter begrudgingly—quite the opposite, in fact; passion will always accompany it in some form. Even though none of our journeys will look the same, they will all begin by accepting the call that is placed on our hearts. That means embracing the unknown and trusting it is worth pursuing because we will discover true fulfillment. Our unique journey of purpose will be found once we assemble each building block together. As we look at them with a new intention, we will see the opportunities to live with real meaning, which are all around us.

SETTING OUR INTENTION

Growing up, I had a strong dislike for reading. Perhaps a strange thing for an author to admit, but it was true. I absolutely despised it. Reading was such a tedious activity for me that I would literally become sleepy every time I tried to read a book. This boredom made literature class in school extremely difficult for me. My reading retention was so low that I would finish a chapter and have no idea what I just read. It was like I said the words on the page in my head, but I paid no attention to their meaning. While my eyes were engaged with the text, my thoughts would instead begin to wander, fixating on other random things. This distracted and disengaged state of mind made me merely go through the motions, completely missing the purpose behind the stories in the book I was reading.

But, after high school, something shifted in my mindset toward books. I had a hunger to develop myself as a leader since starting my business in college. The men I was working with encouraged me to read a list of books to help me grow the skills needed to succeed. That sparked my interest, and I went to buy the first one on the list: *The Dream Giver* by Bruce Wilkinson. Before purchasing it, I sat down to read a few pages in the store, and it struck me with such curiosity that I couldn't put it down. I ended up staying there for hours until I had finished the whole thing. For the first time in my life, a book had captivated me—and I couldn't stop reading. I had a reason to read that I didn't have before.

That experience changed the way I viewed books and gave me a new intention to start reading regularly as I looked for topics that I really desired to grow in. Before, I was aimless, reading books not for myself or because I was interested in them, but out of an obligation to read them for school. But setting a new intention—that I was going to read a book for the purpose of developing myself—allowed me to get the most out of it and truly soak up the meaning within the pages. My relationship with books changed so much that I routinely lingered in bookstores, searching the nonfiction section for inspiring literature.

The relationship I had with books is the same relationship we sometimes have with life—doing things out of obligation, aimlessly moving forward with no particular reason behind what we do. This state of living can feel like we are just drifting along without a sense of direction. It can seem like our lives are boring, leaving us with a hunger for more. We might think we have to do something extreme to break out and find our purpose—something big and bold to have a significant impact. Our path could look like that, but it doesn't have to. The shift to purpose doesn't require us to do something radical. When we simply change the intention behind what we are doing, it can add a new depth of perspective to that activity. We then see the opportunities for purpose within the roles and responsibilities we currently have. This slight adjustment in motivation makes all the difference in changing our level of fulfillment in life.

As we embark on this new journey of purpose, we have a choice to set our intention to look for the opportunities available to us. If we want to experience the fulfillment that comes from living a meaningful life, we need to make a habit of recognizing the ways we can express purpose from here on out. It starts by identifying each building block we discussed—our passion, authenticity, pain, compassion—and then looking for the final one in the form of the unique opportunities we come across, just like Scott. He found his passion for helping the kids of Cambodia by simply living his life and being authentic to who he was. Once the painful experience at the landfill compelled him to do something, he embraced compassion to provide for the first child he met. The change that led him to step into his calling and embrace this unique opportunity was the intention to make a difference with each of his decisions.

We can look at the opportunities in our life with the same type of intention. What stirs within us as we think about the ways we can serve others with our passions, talents, experiences, and love? Asking that question will help us see the ways we can demonstrate purpose. Having this new mindset to make a difference can also impact our view of the things we currently do if we ask ourselves another simple question: "What is my intention?" Answering that question with regard to everything we do, from work to family, friends, hobbies, etc., will give us the chance to bring meaning to our current endeavors by doing them for a reason that's bigger than ourselves.

Simon Sinek, author of the book *Start With Why*, states, "Very few people or companies can clearly articulate WHY they do WHAT they do. When I say WHY, I don't mean to make money—that's a result. By WHY I mean what is your purpose, cause, or belief? WHY does your company exist? WHY do you get out of bed every morning? And WHY should anyone care?" By identifying our reason for doing things and connecting it to a bigger purpose, we can completely transform everything we do.

As we think through the unique opportunities our life has to express purpose, it leaves us with a choice to make that we cannot turn back from. Will we set our intention to accept the call that arises in front of us? Or, will we ignore it and return to living with the sole intent of finding happiness? The choice is clear: To answer the call of purpose, we must exit the pursuit of happiness and assess the deeper meaning behind everything we do. As our awareness increases to the ways in which we can live out our purpose, we will begin to see the unique opportunities within our lives clearly. This new road has immense potential to fulfill us, but we will not realize it if we do not take the final step to propel us into the journey ahead.

Now that we have identified the building blocks we can use to assemble our purpose, it's time to bring all the pieces together. It may take some time as we rearrange them, try out different combinations, and keep looking for that final block of opportunity—but that is the nature of this new journey.

Each area we looked at holds within it clues that will identify expressions of purpose. When we put them together, we will see the collective function they hold that will determine the unique path we take.

In the final section, we will discuss how we can prepare for the road ahead by exploring three components that will propel us forward. We will talk about our faith, actions, and relationships that together will multiply our purpose into the journey ahead. Without each of these factors being present, it would be like unboxing our LEGO set but then leaving the pieces scattered across the floor. Bringing them all together starts with having the faith to see that each piece was put in our life for a reason, which connects us to a bigger story.

ACTIVITY—ASSEMBLING THE BUILDING BLOCKS OF PURPOSE

This exercise will help you see the purpose revealed when taking inventory of the building blocks in your life. Akin to building with LEGOs, there isn't only one way to combine everything but multiple possibilities for living out our purpose. By creating a list for each block, you will recognize the ways they intersect and connect with one another, allowing you to identify practical ways they can form a meaningful expression of purpose in your life.

STEP 1: IDENTIFY YOUR BUILDING BLOCKS
Read through the following questions and write out as many answers that come to your mind. Each one correlates with one of the building blocks of purpose we just discussed.

What core values really fire you up inside? What things are you passionate about? What do you really love doing? (Review the values you circled in the Finding Your Passion section at the end of Chapter 5)

_____

_____

_____

_____

What unique talents, special abilities, or characteristics do you possess? What are you naturally great at?

_____

_____

_____

_____

What breaks your heart? Is there a need, cause, or problem you are aware of that you have compassion for?

_____

_____

_____

_____

What experiences have had a profound impact on your life? What painful events have you gone through that might give you a specific platform?

_____

_____

_____

_____

What opportunities exist that are unique to you? What outlets to impact others are there that would allow you to bring together your passions, talents, heart, and experience?

_____

_____

_____

_____

STEP 2: REVIEW AND REFLECT

Look over your answers and invite a trusted friend or family member who knows you well to do the same. Ask them to review your responses and identify any other things they see in you that should be added. These lists are not set in stone. In fact, think of them like a working whiteboard that you can reflect on and add to over time as things change.

STEP 3: FIND THE INTERSECTION

Brainstorm ideas for how each of these categories intersects with one another. Without any judgments, list out any ideas for how they can all be combined and used together. Then summarize your intention below by picking the one idea that gives you the most energy to express your purpose going forward.

How might your purpose come together from these building blocks to impact the world or others around you?

_____

_____

_____

_____

PART III

THE JOURNEY

10

FAITH: THE PURPOSE MULTIPLIER

———

*"I cry out to God Most High, to God
who fulfills his purpose for me."*

—PSALM 57:2

It is no accident you are reading this book. In fact, it is no accident it was written. Several events had to take place to give me the inspiration, ideas, and time to write it. I believe the fine line that led me to this point wasn't because of my cleverness or luck. It was because God had a plan that brought it all together. I know I am not alone in my journey because I can look back and see how so many people came into my life at just the right time. It feels like I am a part of a bigger story—a narrative written to connect my life with God and with others. That belief has allowed me to see how everything I've gone through was intentionally preparing me for where I am today.

Each of the five building blocks we explored in the previous section will show us ideas about what living with our purpose looks like in real life. They give us a practical view of where we can find specific expressions of our purpose—the passions we have, the talents we possess, the experiences we've gone through, the people we love, and the unique opportunities available to us. In the following three chapters, we are going to look at three areas to multiply our purpose and move forward onto the road ahead.

Each will play a particularly important role in helping us maximize our purpose and find fulfillment along the way. As we zero in on how we can best express our purpose, there is an important component that will sustain us on our journey and bring purpose to everything we do: our faith.

WHAT WE BELIEVE

Faith, by itself, can lead us to tremendous purpose by touching everything in our lives. It has the power to multiply our impact and bring a deeper level of meaning to all that we do. The starting line of faith is what we believe. Our beliefs are the foundation of our faith in anything, whether that is faith in the future, faith in ourselves, or faith in God. What we believe to be true will dictate how we act during times of uncertainty. It's important we examine this because life is full of unknowns and things that are out of our control—especially as we start our journey of purpose. How we respond in the face of uncertainty is a direct reflection of our faith. Do we believe everything happens for a reason or that our life is nothing more than a series of random events?

In either case, it doesn't change our control over the events that happen to us, but it does dictate our response to them. If our lives are nothing more than acts of randomness, then it makes us view ourselves as either being lucky or unlucky, depending on if we get outcomes that are favorable or unfavorable. But seeing our circumstances that way isn't helpful. We risk losing hope in the future if we get into a season of difficulty and feel like our luck has run out. Our focus then remains fixed on the painful events we face and causes us to feel trapped as victims of our circumstances. Instead of dwelling on things outside our control, we need to focus on a factor that we can control—how we respond.

Our response to life events that happen to us is a direct reflection of our beliefs. What if, instead, we believe everything happens for a reason? That no matter what events come our way, there is some sort of meaning behind them—what difference would that make in our lives? Even if we are not quite sure if that is true, the possibility that it might be will cause us to do our own investigating. Whether the circumstances we face are good or bad, it will prompt us to ask questions of each one, which will redirect our focus. We will then look for the reason behind the things that happen to us and see the response it is leading us to make. Maybe it is all preparing us for something much bigger.

If we believe in the possibility that everything happens for a reason, it will prompt us to look at the events in our lives in a new light. If nothing is random chance, then there must be something or someone that brings order and meaning to it all. That leads us to what we must consider next: we are not alone. Does our faith rest solely on believing in ourselves and our own ability to navigate the road ahead, or do we believe

God is with us and has brought us to this point in our lives for a reason?

BELIEVING IN A BIGGER STORY

Louis Zamperini faced several near-death experiences during his lifetime. He turned to God in his most desperate moments of need, but once he was out of harm's way, he went on to live life on his own. Only when he fully believed that he was a part of God's bigger narrative did his life transform for a greater purpose—one that would give him the ability to do the impossible.

It started in 1940, during the outbreak of World War II, when Louis decided to join the US Army Air force as a B-24 bomber. Three years later, with several flying missions under his belt, he received orders to go on a search and rescue assignment to look for a missing aircraft crew. Mid-flight, as they were conducting their search, their plane suddenly had a mechanical failure and crashed down into the ocean 850 miles south of Oahu, Hawaii. Eight people died instantly, leaving Louis and two others stranded at sea.

Left with little food and no water, Louis and his two remaining crewmates fought for survival against starvation and dehydration. They saved rainwater whenever they could, killed birds to use as bait to catch fish, and fought off daily attacks from sharks that threatened to capsize their raft. One of the most intense battles they faced at sea came from a severe storm that threatened to sink them. The storm relentlessly poured water into their boat as they frantically bailed it out to avoid sinking. After hours of labor, Louis cried out to God, "Get me home alive, God, and I'll seek you and serve you." They managed to stay afloat that night, and after forty-seven days at sea, their raft eventually drifted alongshore to the Marshall Islands.[54]

Louis's delight in arriving at land was short-lived. The Japanese Navy immediately captured him as a prisoner of war. Taken to one of the most grueling POW camps, he met their head corporal, nicknamed "the Bird," who made it his special mission to single out Louis and repeatedly beat him. At one point, he hit him so hard in the head that it left Louis deaf in one ear for several weeks. The brutal torture he received haunted him with terrible nightmares. Every day he woke up with the constant dread that today might be the day he dies. In the depth of his hopelessness, he prayed to God again and made a deal to serve him with his life if he would only bring him home alive.

Louis endured two years in the prison camp, and at the end of the war, he finally made it home. After his return, he met a woman named Cynthia Applewhite and proceeded to marry her the following year. Louis tried to move on with his life but continued to be tormented with nightmares. He had forgotten about his prayers to God and became bitter and deeply angry toward his captors. Louie felt like the only way forward was to return to Japan to find the Bird and kill him. His nightmares become so severe to the point that he once woke up in the middle of the night to find himself in the process of strangling his sleeping wife, thinking she was the Bird. He turned to alcohol to help him sleep, but it only made things worse, leaving Cynthia to want to get a divorce.

Concerned by the goings-on, one of Cynthia's friends invited her and Louis to a Billy Graham Crusade. After hearing the message about forgiveness, Cynthia no longer wanted to leave him. The sudden change of heart prompted Louis, who left the sermon the day before, to return for the last day.

As Louis listened to the message that time, one line abruptly caught his attention: *"What God asks of men is faith."* Hearing that caused Louis to remember the promise of faith that he had made to God on the raft and in prison. "God kept his promise," Louis said in his biography, *Unbroken*. "You know, he brought me home alive, and here I am turning my back on him." At that moment, he got up and walked back to the prayer room and asked God to forgive him as he placed his faith in Jesus Christ.

Louis felt a calmness and peace wash over him as he prayed, and he knew he was done trying to get by on his own strength. He also felt a feeling of forgiveness replace the anger he had within him toward all his prison guards, including the Bird. Returning home that night, he did not have a nightmare—for the first time in four years. His marriage and his life had turned down the path of healing.

Louis found a sense of purpose in sharing his story of faith with others. Instead of returning for revenge, he traveled back to Japan to share the message of God's forgiveness and the story of how God saved his life. He personally met with and forgave many of the Japanese guards he once hated for beating him and were now behind bars for war crimes. The Bird refused to meet with him, but Louis wrote him a letter detailing his story and how he was able to forgive him too, saying, "Love replaced the hate I had for you."[55]

Without faith, the purpose within Louis's story couldn't be unlocked until he believed that he was part of a bigger narrative and placed his trust in God. Then he could see the meaning within his story and have an impact on the world and those around him.

EXPLORING OUR BELIEFS

Without the belief that God exists connecting us to a bigger narrative, we are left alone to rely on ourselves or construct a set of beliefs to make sense of life. This course of action may work for a time, but at some point, we are likely to encounter events that are out of our control or that we cannot explain. How we respond when that happens will shape the future of our lives—do we rely more on our own efforts or lean into our faith? Just like Louis, many people turn to God in their most profound time of need, amid their pain, only to forget him once they've gotten out safe on the other side. But God is still there, always present with us, patiently waiting for us to acknowledge him so he can transform whatever we've gone through for a bigger purpose.

As we consider the belief that everything happens for a reason and connects us to a bigger story that God is writing, are there any doubts that come into your mind? Not answering the questions that arise will end any chance of understanding what is true. We must not get discouraged if that is where we find ourselves. Instead, we must simply believe that faith is worth exploring—no matter how many questions we have or how difficult they may be to answer. Because sometimes, our doubts will be the very thing that leads us to believe in God. That is what happened to one of the most prominent atheists of the twentieth century: C.S. Lewis.

Clive Staples Lewis was raised going to church regularly, but when he was ten years old, his mother suddenly died of cancer. That tragic experience destroyed any belief he had in God. After praying relentlessly for God to save his mother, Lewis declared, "He [God] is like a person who never acknowledges one's letters and so, in time, one comes to the conclusion either that he does not exist or that you have got the address wrong."

By the time Lewis was sixteen years old, he was a devout atheist who openly professed about it to everyone. "I believe in no God," Lewis wrote in a letter to a friend. "Why would any intelligent person want to believe in a bogey who is prepared to torture me for ever and ever?" That disbelief was reinforced when he went off to fight in World War I. He witnessed the horrors of war, including the death of his best friend, which made him more devout in his atheist beliefs.[56]

Lewis finished his education at Oxford after the war and became a teacher. He grew a deep passion for literature and reading. Some of the books he read were by various Christian authors and sparked a curiosity within him. As he continued to hold onto his beliefs that God didn't exist, Lewis realized it contradicted his love for the elements he so deeply admired in literature—namely, the beauty and meaning each story possessed.

If atheism were true, it meant that the world was void of all meaning because everything was random. Lewis explored other worldviews and researched various beliefs. His search left him realizing that it was actually hard to argue with the theory that some kind of God, in fact, existed. "Atheism turns out to be too simple," he said. "If the whole universe has no meaning, we should never have found out that it has no meaning."[57]

His relentless search for answers eventually led to his belief in God and caused him to write one of the most influential books about the Christian faith: *Mere Christianity*. The explanations and arguments he gives that God is real are grounded in reason and his experiences because of his quest to get to the bottom of what he believed. He found that in his journey through life, his deep desire for something more was one of the strongest indications that God existed, noting, "If I find in myself a desire which no experience in this world can satisfy, the most probable explanation is that I was made for another world."

Faith is very simply defined in the dictionary as "a complete trust or confidence in someone or something." It may seem reasonable, then, to think that the opposite of that definition is a lack of belief or doubt in something, but in reality, our doubts don't compromise our faith. The opposite of faith is not having doubts or being unsure in what we believe—it's not caring one way or the other. Displaying indifference or apathy causes us to think answering any faith-related questions is not essential, which produces an attitude that doesn't care to explore what we believe or don't and instead leaves us relying on ourselves. If we give up on looking for the answers to the doubts we have, then our faith never has a chance to grow.

The conclusion that Lewis came to about what he believed was only made possible because he never stopped searching for what he believed. The tragic events he faced in life were difficult to deal with and left him doubting that God existed. But his longings kept pushing him to look for answers to his questions about faith and life. His persistent desires led him to see that God was real and that he was created for a purpose that was not of this world.

BELIEVING IN ANOTHER WORLD

At the beginning of this book, we talked about the shared experience people have of feeling like something is missing.

I described it as a void—a space in my heart that I couldn't satisfy. This desire for something we can't identify in our life is what often starts us on the road toward the pursuit of happiness as we seek to fulfill our cravings for more. But what if these relentless longings we have are simply a sign that we were created for something else entirely? Just like Lewis discovered, what if our never-ending desires are pointing us to find our purpose beyond this world? Many of the principles in this book can lead us to find purpose without a Christian worldview, but it would be incomplete if I did not ask these questions to point out where I believe true purpose is found.

I believe this void or emptiness we often feel results from sin in our life that is separating us from God and is impossible to fix on our own. In order to redeem this part of ourselves, we must have faith and accept the price God paid to cleanse us from our sin by sending his Son to die in our place. When we ask for his forgiveness for our sins, we change the destination of our journey. Not only do our souls become redeemed, but it transforms our entire story as we become connected to the narrative that God is writing—the purpose and identity he gives us. Then we can begin to live for eternity and consider the legacy we will leave behind.

Having the faith to believe that life on earth is only the beginning of our journey opens up a whole new dimension of our purpose. It is possible to live with significance and positively impact people without any faith that God or eternity exists. But the deep longings we have are proof that we are spiritual beings consisting of more than the flesh and bones that make up our bodies. If we only focus our purpose on life in this world, we will fail to meet the spiritual needs of our souls. There is an unexplained realm of pain in our lives that can only be healed by connecting our purpose to the one God has for us. When we do that, we see that faith in God is the purpose multiplier. He creates and expands our significance, allowing our impact to carry on long after we are gone. This should prompt us to ask ourselves what we believe and what kind of legacy we will leave behind.

As you contemplate that, consider how you want people to remember you. What do you want to be said of you at your funeral or written on your tombstone? When we build our purpose with eternity in mind, we will focus on the things that will impact people after we are gone. It will motivate us to assemble the building blocks of purpose in our lives in such a way that they will inspire the next generation. Purpose with an eternal mindset can be passed on like a torch, carried along in the souls of others long after we die.

Having the faith to believe in something bigger than ourselves is a critical first step to multiplying our purpose, but it will not do us any good if we don't take action. In the next chapter, we are going to explore how to take our beliefs and do something with them to launch our purpose into the world.

11

ACTION: THE IGNITION OF PURPOSE

———

"Small deeds done are better than
great deeds planned."

—PETER MARSHALL

It takes about 76,000 gallons of fuel to send a rocket to the moon. But before igniting this massive amount of stored energy, there is a long list of system checks that needs to first be completed. If one element required is missing or not functioning correctly, the team can't launch. If they tried to push through ignoring these checks, they would compromise the mission and risk failure.

Before NASA sent the first man to the moon in 1969, they needed to have a deep sense of conviction that the mission the crew was working on was worth the risk. Doing something that has never been done before carries many unknowns, but the team built up their confidence through studying what they knew and building toward launch day, one step at a time. The zeal they needed to bring everything together came from the burning desire and excitement to make history by being the first to land on the moon. There was a lot of emotion behind pushing that final button to ignite the rockets into space as they trusted their work had prepared the crew to be the first to ever land on the moon. We need to have these same elements for us to take action.

CONVICTION IN THE MISSION

When we see an opportunity, we have to be convinced that taking action is necessary—that it is worth the risk to act instead of doing nothing. Such faith can arise if we think the cause is worthy or someone is in real need of our help. When we are entirely confident that our action is required, we feel obligated to act. We feel like it is our responsibility to address the need that has just been brought to our attention. That level of conviction creates a clarity of mind within us, which shows us what we must do. This type of conviction is something Jake Wood exemplified on multiple occasions during his life.

Jake received a full-ride football scholarship to the University of Wisconsin as an offensive lineman. During his freshman year, he witnessed on television the horrific events of September 11. Watching the Twin Towers fall sparked a desire within him to fight back. He continued with his college football career as the US invasion of Iraq began. In 2004, during his senior year of college, one of his role models in football, NFL player Pat Tillman, was killed. That event sparked a nerve in Jake to take action.

Pat was a well-known football player in the Arizona Cardinals. He, like Jake, saw the attack on the Twin Towers, and it stirred him to retaliate. In 2002, Pat turned down a $3.6 million football contract to join the US Army. Seeing him live with such passion and assertiveness in life as he gave up his NFL career to serve his country was deeply inspiring to Jake. "It just struck me that this man lived with conviction and paid the ultimate sacrifice, and I realized that I wanted to live a life like that." The following year, Jake joined the Marines.[58]

He served two combat tours in Iraq and Afghanistan in four years. After Jake completed his service and returned home, he witnessed another devastating event on television: the aftermath of the 2010 Haiti earthquake that ravaged their country. The images of destruction he saw reminded him very clearly of his experience in Afghanistan. Just like during 9/11, what he witnessed on television upset him and compelled him to take action to help. Jake called one of his fellow veterans, and they decided to fly down to Haiti to link up with a group to assist in the relief efforts.

After first flying to the Dominican Republic, they crossed the border into Haiti. Immediately it felt like they were in a war zone, and they realized their former combat experience uniquely equipped them for this. As people frantically searched for loved ones amid the chaos, they remained calm. Using their military training, they set up medical triages to apply first aid to the injured. After treating a child's leg that had been severely damaged, Jake looked down at his hands covered in blood and realized something profound—*"These hands weren't just trained for war, they were trained to help, to heal, and to serve my fellow man."*[59]

The idea was born to start a disaster relief organization using the skills and training of fellow veterans to serve communities around the world after major natural disasters. Jake founded Team Rubicon with this conviction and deployed teams worldwide to aid in relief efforts. Veterans joined these teams as they willingly accepted the call to serve their fellow man with their unique military training. What Jake didn't realize at the time was how this effort to help others would profoundly change the lives of the veterans themselves.

In 2011, Jake lost one of his best friends, Clay Hunt, to suicide. Jake had served with Clay overseas and was the best man at his wedding. Clay had been the victim of PTSD and depression as he wrestled with trying to adapt to civilian life after his combat tours. "What was really tragic," Jake said, "… was that Clay didn't kill himself because of what happened to us in Iraq and in Afghanistan. No, Clay killed himself because of what he lost when he came home—he lost his sense of purpose, he lost his sense of community, and he lost his sense of self."[60]

Jake realized that those were three very simple things Team Rubicon could provide to veterans while deploying their skills to serve disaster-stricken communities around the world. This discovery added fuel to his mission as he sought to help as many veterans as possible by restoring their sense of purpose. The organization grew from an initial team of eight to over 120,000 volunteers today. Since 2010, Team Rubicon has been deployed on over 650 disaster missions across the world. The training that prepared so many for combat was now being repurposed to heal and rebuild disaster-stricken communities and the very veterans who roll up their sleeves to serve them.[61]

Jake's conviction was the energy that led him to live with purpose during each critical intersection of his life. It gave him the clarity of mind to see a clear action step that he knew he needed to take. There was no doubt in his mind concerning what he needed to do. The strength of this conviction allowed him to know exactly how he should respond. He knew he needed to join the Marines when he was inspired by Pat Tillman. And he knew he needed to go to Haiti when he saw the destruction the earthquake caused. There were several defining moments in Jake's life where his resolve propelled him forward to live with purpose. But this wasn't the only element present—without the confidence to act, he wouldn't have followed through on his conviction.

CONFIDENCE IN MOTION

Conviction alone isn't enough. We not only have to be sure that our action is required, but we need to believe in our ability to carry it out. We need to possess the confidence that we have what it takes to act in even the most minor way possible. Having such trust in our abilities can come as we draw on our prior experience or talents, but it can also develop as we simply start doing something. The slightest step forward can assure us of our ability to take another. If we believe we are not qualified or doubt we have the right skills, then our action will get stopped in its tracks. To overcome the self-doubt that causes us to question ourselves, we must identify the smallest first step we can take that we do have confidence in, instead of ignoring our conviction altogether. This incremental process will help us avoid the fear that can creep in and cause us to overthink and delay taking action.

What if I fail, or what if I don't have what it takes? What if I embarrass myself or let people down? These questions arise from fear, which can become an extremely paralyzing emotion that hinders our ability to act. If we give in to these questions, it can completely shut down any movement toward action. But what would happen if we listened to our fears? What if we gave in and did nothing? We would miss out on a potentially life-changing experience. We can use the powerful emotion of fear against itself to help propel us to act by changing the narrative we tell ourselves. When we become more afraid of not doing anything than we are of failing, we will take action.

If our self-limiting fears are not addressed, they will lead us into confusion. We begin to question ourselves and become clouded in our judgment that we are unsure of the right thing to do or the best move to take first. Confusion can leave us in disarray and is much more subtle than fear. It's not an emotion, so there isn't energy behind it that can be used against itself. It is more akin to a vacuum that sucks away the vigor we do have, leaving us less and less sure what to do. Dwelling on our confusion will spiral us into apathy, where we become so distraught that we think it's just better not to care anymore—at least then we won't suffer from the agony of indecision.

Confusion leads us to make excuses and procrastinate. If we reason that we will just do something tomorrow or once we get a few other things done first, we run the risk of our conviction growing stale. We can become overwhelmed with other priorities and convince ourselves that we just don't have the time. Or we may fall into the pit of analysis paralysis— repeatedly remunerating about what to actually do. These thoughts chip away at our confidence, causing us to question ourselves further. To overcome this, we can bring some urgency to our actions and learn from Benjamin

Franklin, who once said, "Don't put off until tomorrow what you can do today."

We may not have the background that Jake did that gave him the confidence to jump into the aftermath of the earthquake in Haiti, and that's okay. It may not be our call to act on, but that cannot become a recurring excuse that removes us from acting on anything. We need to find what we do have the confidence to do and act on that as soon as possible, no matter how small it may be. There is no act too small for our first step because any action is energy that gets us moving forward. According to Newton's first law, an object in motion stays in motion, and an object at rest remains at rest. This law of momentum can be used to take one small step after another that will grow into something truly impactful. But in order to overcome the initial inertia, there needs to be some sort of energy combustion—something that will spark us to take that first step.

IGNITING ACTION

When we put ourselves in the middle of the pain and the need that we are witnessing, it will engage our emotions and give us a kindling of energy to ignite our will to act. The feeling we experience can vary depending on the situation—anger, sadness, fear, excitement, etc. A common one is righteous anger, which results from becoming deeply upset that something should be done to fix a particular problem. Like Jake Wood responding to the call to join the Marines or go to Haiti, the final component of combustion erupts when we witness an injustice occurring, for which we are deeply troubled by and see as our personal responsibility to act upon. The emotional response we have is the spark of energy needed to kick-start our actions.

After my freshman year of college, I decided that I was done with school. The online business I started was booming, and I wanted to commit to it full-time to reach its maximum potential. I moved back to my hometown, got an apartment, and got a job selling online ad space while I continued to build my business. My family wasn't happy with my decision to drop out of college. They tried relentlessly to convince me to go back every chance they got, but it always fell on deaf ears. I wouldn't even entertain the option. I was so focused on building my business and convinced this was the right path for me.

About two years later, sales at my online marketing company stopped growing, and my interest in selling ad space online fizzled out. I had learned in that time how much I loved helping people and started looking for other jobs. We had a friend of the family who was a financial advisor who piqued my interest to investigate that as an option. It seemed like the perfect fit that combined my analytical skills, desire to help people, and flexibility to prioritize a future family someday. So, I decided to shut down my business and pursue a career to become a financial advisor.

I landed an interview at an investment firm in Chicago after a friend who worked there referred me for a job. It was an ideal spot to start my new career. I was really excited everything was coming together. At the end of the first day of the interview process, I met with Jim, the president of the company, and handed him my résumé. He was impressed with my experience in sales and with my business, but after a few minutes, he looked at me and asked, "Can I be honest with you and give you some advice?" I, of course, agreed, eager to know what he was going to say. "I would hire you today except for one thing: you don't have a degree," he said as he gave me guidance on how I should return to school and study finance.

I had heard it so many times before—you need to finish school. But this time, it really made me upset. I was mad that finishing school was standing in my way to getting this job. My attitude flipped from being so against needing a degree to thinking, "Fine, I'll go back to school—and not only that, but I will take classes year-round to do it as fast as possible." This combustion of emotion ignited the energy within that propelled me to act. I left his office that day in November and sent my parents this email the following day:

"Since leaving the interview, I have put a lot of thought into what Jim (the president) said and what I want to do. I am not sure why this time after hearing "you should get your degree," it is resonating the way it is in me – well I think I do. I feel moved, called to attack this challenge, and I am still in this angry but fired up mode ... so I have decided to start classes in January to work towards a Finance degree at a school near home."

It didn't matter how many truly well-meaning family members tried to convince me to finish school by attempting to appeal to me with common sense and logic. I wasn't going back to finish my degree until I experienced the combustion of emotion that ignited me into action. This final element appeared in me once I made it personal. In this case, not having a degree was the very thing that was keeping me from living out my purpose. That realization activated my emotional engine, which sparked me to finish school and tackle whatever obstacle was standing in the way of where I felt called to go.

BUILDING MOMENTUM

When you look at the way you think about your life's purpose, do you have the conviction, confidence, and combustion of emotion that will lead you to take action? When we have the faith to believe choosing to live with purpose is worth it, it will give us the conviction we need to change our approach. If we boil down the principles to one simple act we can take, we will have confidence in that first step. As we do that, we can make the needs of others personal and let our emotions move us to actually change. Together, this will build the momentum that will carry us forward one decision at a time.

The foundational mindset we established at the beginning of this book showed us that our capacity for purpose is not something we need to acquire but something already present in our abilities. As we look to take action in the world, we aren't trying to achieve something new. We are taking action to give out of what we already have. Therefore, we shouldn't be intimidated or afraid of failure; we must simply take that which we possess—our talents, abilities, experiences, opportunities, etc.—and use them to serve the needs of others that come to our attention along our journey. You have already taken the first step by reading this book. Now you must just follow it up by bringing your awareness of purpose with you as you live your life—working with others, talking with family, going to school, hanging with friends, etc. As you become conscious of the things you do daily, you will recognize opportunities to serve others—thus extending your purpose through the people in your life.

This shift in our focus helps us build momentum as we move forward. It primes the pump for our conviction to start the chain reaction that will propel us into making a difference in the world. As you think through the building blocks of purpose in your life, what call to action do you feel convicted about implementing? Is there a specific expression of purpose you feel compelled to share with others? As you think through what that might look like, write down one simple task you can do this week to move toward expressing it in your life. Clarify your intention and write it out somewhere you will see it each day as a reminder to keep living with purpose wherever you go.

Taking action may be scary or uncertain, but by realizing we have already taken the first step, we can keep the momentum going by looking for opportunities to express purpose in our lives. Having that awareness will help us take the next step, and the next, to propel us into this new way of living. We will then realize that the target of our purpose is people. In the next chapter, we will explore the purpose the people in our lives have and see that relationships are the avenue through which we impact the world.

12

PEOPLE: THE LEGACY
OF PURPOSE

———

"Treasure your relationships, not your possessions."

—ANTHONY J. D'ANGELO

Each of the stories we explored in the previous chapters involved an experience where someone discovered a need that led them to make a difference in another person's life. People were the focal point and recipient of each expression of purpose. Through encounters with others, particular needs became evident, and the opportunity to do something became clear. As we focus on how we are going to live with meaning, it will sharpen our awareness of those we interact with each day—the people we are closest to and even those we haven't met yet.

When we walk in our purpose alongside the people in our lives, the opportunities we have to make a difference in the world become clearer and clearer. Our awareness of others grows as we see that our energy is best spent focused on the impact we can have through the people we interact with each day. As we look for such opportunities, it will often draw our attention to those right in front of us, who we are best equipped to serve. True fulfillment on our journey will come as we value people enough to lean into new and existing relationships to connect on a deeper level with those around us. That is the context through which we will see the way forward and have a meaningful impact on the world. When we do, we will have an opportunity to pass on the torch of purpose by leaving a legacy that will carry on in the hearts of others.

As we look more specifically at the people in our own lives, we will find that each one of them gives us meaning. With all our relationships, we have a role or responsibility that comes along with it. Friend, spouse, parent, brother, sister, employee, etc., are all various roles that describe our relation to others and provide a unique context for us to impact their lives. When we focus on our purpose and take the time to be present with people, we will discover the meaning found in each of our relationships and the opportunity to express our purpose in serving them.

Realizing the importance of people in our life will help us focus on the impact we can have through our relationships. I discovered this after experiencing the emptiness that exists when our ability to connect with others is interrupted. Living through the COVID-19 pandemic showed me how my sense of purpose is closely tied to the connections with the people in my life, which changed how I thought about my interactions with others.

THE IMPORTANCE OF PEOPLE

It was November 2020, about eight months into the global pandemic. All my regular daily and weekly routines—going to the gym, the office, and to church—were canceled because of the national quarantine implemented to slow the spread of COVID-19. While I was extremely thankful to still have my health, job, and family, I felt increasingly isolated as the winter set in. Living in quarantine by myself in my one-bedroom apartment felt like solitary confinement. I had not seen anyone in over a month, which made my life seem so empty and mundane. My anxiety levels were steadily rising throughout the year, and the combination of everything led me to a breaking point.

Turning to God, I leaned on my faith for comfort, but I felt a sense of dread and uneasiness each day that made it hard to function. My anxiety became physical manifestations of pressure in my body. There was a weight on my chest and a tightness in my throat that I had never experienced before. I was sad, bored, and growing more anxious by the day. If I sat still, I could feel the heaviness of my heart as it pounded louder and louder with each beat. At times it even seemed like it was fluttering. I had never encountered anxiety like this where I didn't understand where it was coming from. I just felt depressed, tired, and worthless—like I was meaninglessly drifting along in life.

I scheduled some time to talk with my counselor, and he encouraged me to journal what I was experiencing. Writing down my feelings was therapeutic. As I finished getting it all out, I read over what I had written. In looking at my emotions objectively, I realized they were coming from deep within a part of me that was starving. In the same way that my stomach would yell at me if I didn't eat food for a week or a month, my body and emotions were yelling at me with the pangs of hunger for human connection.

I did a lot that year to find my purpose, solidify my faith in God, and even put my purpose into action by starting to write this book, but this hunger revealed I still lacked something. At first, it felt like the perfect year to begin this writing project and do something meaningful with all the extra free time I had. But then the irony of feeling so purposeless while trying to write a book on purpose set in and became incredibly defeating. All my days seemed so meaningless as I did the same thing week after week—how do I help others live with purpose when it feels like purpose has eluded me? I spent countless hours at home behind the computer working all day and then writing all evening. I was excited to have found such an opportunity to share my passion for finding purpose, but as I lost my connection with people, I lost my sense of purpose.

Thankfully, our family decided to still have our usual gatherings in person for the holidays that year. The time of being physically present with each other over Thanksgiving and Christmas were two of the most life-giving weekends I had experienced all year. I focused on cherishing the time together and took nothing for granted. My hunger pangs slowly subsided as seeing everyone in person restored my connection to the people in my life. That experience showed me the vital role that people play in our lives. It reminded me why I started writing this book in the first place—not for the prestige of becoming an author, but to have an impact on the lives of others.

As I thought about the way books had played a role in changing my life, it restored my sense of purpose to consider the potential impact my writing could have on others. Even though I had found my purpose in this season of my life, I wasn't able to sustain it without keeping the activity of writing connected with the people it would one day impact. With that focus clear in my mind, it renewed my sense of meaning and got me through my time of isolation.

Looking back, I am thankful I listened to the anxiety I experienced. It took a pandemic for me to truly see just how important people are to our purpose. We need others in our lives to connect and interact with and to give us an opportunity to share our talents, abilities, and experiences with. In a world without people, one's life would feel so empty and deprived of meaning—just like living life in quarantine. It is easy to realize this when we are alone and isolated, but will we still value relationships when our interactions with others are abundant, or will we take them for granted?

Sometimes we only realize the true value of something when it is no longer present in our lives. It's easy to notice how essential oxygen is when we are suffocating or holding our breath underwater, but when the airflow is freely flowing, do we even think about breathing? Or are we just on autopilot? As we bring our attention to the priority we place on our relationships, it will help us see the things that prevent us from genuinely connecting with others. Realizing what causes us to go into autopilot mode will help us stay connected to others and avoid getting burnt out.

The biggest thing that prohibits us from connecting with people is being too busy. Our preoccupation with work or the next item to cross off our to-do list can keep us distracted from the life-giving relationships around us. Even if we find our work extremely enjoyable and energizing, the way to sustain that level of satisfaction in the future is to stay connected to the people in our lives. If we can develop a balanced pace in our schedules, it will allow us to be with others in the present moment and avoid getting burnt out in the future.

SETTING OUR PACE

Shonda Rhimes was extremely busy and often completely burned out being the executive producer and screenwriter for *Grey's Anatomy*, *Private Practice*, and *Scandal*. She worked fifteen-hour days and many times worked through the weekend while also juggling her responsibilities as a mother to her three kids at home. She absolutely loved her work, but her life was heading in an unsustainable direction that eventually depleted all the joy she found in her career. The things that used to get Shonda excited no longer gave her energy, yet she continued to put her work first above everything else.

Looking for a way to shake things up and regain her energy, she tried an experiment for a year by saying yes to everything that scared her, no matter what. This experiment allowed her to realize all the things she was missing out on by not saying yes to them before. One of her biggest realizations came when her daughter asked her a question that ended up changing the energy she had for her career and all her priorities. That one remarkably simple question was, "Momma, will you play with me?"

Shonda was heading out the door, already late for work, but remembering her commitment to saying yes, she stopped and agreed to play with her daughter. The playtime that followed was just like any other time they had played together, but as she reflected in that moment, she decided that whatever she had going on from then on, she was going to say yes anytime one of her kids asked her to play—no matter what. It became a rule, a law, that she followed. As she prioritized spending time with the people she valued most, joy returned to her life, and the creative energy needed for work flowed again. That time of playing with her kids provided a newfound vitality that made her more productive at her job than if she had spent the extra hour working.[62]

Shonda had discovered the importance of saying yes to her relationships, which allowed her to prioritize the activities and people that gave her energy. Learning to play with her kids was not easy for her to do. She never said no to working—she was so conditioned to always put her career first. But slowly, she learned to create space in her schedule to be with her kids and unplug from the demands of her job. Even though she absolutely loved her career, it disconnected her from the people she cared about most. In order to find a sustainable pace, she needed to be reminded to connect with her most cherished relationships in life to give her the energy to do her best work. Taking the time to intentionally spend with her kids was the necessary rhythm she needed to stay connected to the relationships that motivated her to work so hard in the first place.

Anyone who has run a marathon could tell you the importance of knowing your running pace. The time it takes to comfortably complete a mile is important to know when you have twenty-six of them to run. If all our energy is expended in the first mile, we will never make it to the finish line. The same is true as we embark on the journey ahead. As we realize the critical role the people in our life have, we can make them a priority when we find our sustainable pace of life. That will keep us from burning out along the way and give us the ability to see and connect with the people we come across every day.

Our schedules dictate the speed of our life—how frequently we have things to do and the number of activities we cram into each of our days. We will be able to set the proper pace of our lives by gaining control of our calendars. When we are mindful of the things we say yes to and pay attention to the things we need to say no to, we can prioritize what really matters. The direction we take in living with purpose will be determined by what we allow and don't allow on our schedules. It is important that we bring our new intention into each of these decisions so we can develop discernment in learning when we need to say no to someone or something.

Saying no can be difficult because we never want to offend or let anyone down. But the reality is that saying no to the activities or people that drain us can enable us to help others more effectively. It will declutter our schedule enough to say yes to the people who bring us life and fuel us further along in our journey. The reason saying no can be so difficult is not only because we don't want to hurt anyone's feelings, but because oftentimes, we don't feel like we have a good enough reason to say no. However, when we look at it from the perspective that overextending ourselves admittedly hurts our relationships, it will give us the ability to better protect our schedules going forward.

Pursuing purpose doesn't mean we fill up our time with as many things as possible that align with our calling by saying yes to every opportunity to give, help, and serve. Being selective in saying yes to the right people or things and saying no to the others will allow us to find our sustainable pace in life to be able to truly connect with the people all around us. As we prioritize our relationships, we will see that our pursuit isn't about arriving at any particular destination; rather, it's a journey of seeing the purpose in each interaction along our way.

What do you need to say no to so that you can start saying yes to the right relationships in your life? Bringing this mindset intentionally into our journey of purpose will take us places we may never have gone before. As we connect our purpose with people, it will bring us life and help sustain us moving forward to continue our journey for our lifetime and beyond. What we will find as we do this is that sharing our resources to serve people is contagious. Making time to connect with others as we live with purpose will likely inspire them to do the same thing. That will give us the opportunity to pass on the torch of our legacy through their lives.

PASSING THE TORCH

One of my favorite hobbies is going on solo hiking and camping trips to explore the great outdoors. There is something incredibly peaceful about finding solitude alone in the mountains. But even though I usually start each hike by myself, I always come across other people walking along the same trail. That has led to many conversations and meeting new people as we journey together for miles ahead to our destination. Being on the same trail made it natural to connect and get to know each other. Our shared adventure allowed us to go from strangers to friends in no time because of the instant bond we had in our love for hiking and being at the same place; at the same time.

It was always a great sense of accomplishment to have reached the destination at the end of a hike with extraordinary views. But it was the people I met and connected with

along the way that really gave me purpose in my journey—
not only from sharing the adventure with those I was hiking
with on the way up; but also from all the people I would cross
paths with on the way down. Being able to share the experience I gained with other hikers who were headed to the same
point I was returning from provided me an opportunity to
help them by giving guidance to navigate the trail ahead. I
was able to pass on what I had learned to encourage them
for their journey. These encounters added a deeper level of
meaning to each of my adventures.

We may not find ourselves on the same hiking trail in
the mountains, but we are all on the same trail of life. We
cross paths with people every day who are heading in various
directions. Some are going to places we have just returned
from, while others are going alongside us to the same one.
At the end of the day, we will find true fulfillment in life, not
in our accomplishments of arriving at our destination, but
instead in the connections that we make with others along
the way.

Focusing on people is easier when we recognize the shared
adventure of life we are on together, which gives us a bond,
no matter how different our lives may seem. As we realize
what we have in common, it will give us an opportunity to
pass on what we have learned to others. The relationships we
have and the ones we have yet to establish will provide us the
chance to share our time, treasure, or talents to help people in
their journey. Looking for the difference we can make in the
lives of everyone we know and meet is how we leave a legacy.

How intentional are you in genuinely connecting with
the people in your life? Who are you especially capable of
helping in their journey? What would it look like to take your
purpose and leave a legacy in the lives of others?

We may not set out to change the world, but we can make a difference in the life of at least one person. When we make people the focal point through which we express our purpose, we have an opportunity to pass on the torch to the next generation. Our relationships are the avenue through which we can leave a legacy of purpose that will live on in the hearts and minds of others. As we become more aware of the people in our lives and intentionally connect with them, we will experience true fulfillment that will sustain us on our journey. It is not about reaching some destination of a grander purpose but recognizing the joy that comes from the meaning found in genuinely connecting with others along the way. Focus on living each day, each moment, looking for the opportunity to pass on the torch of our legacy by making a difference in the lives of those we touch. When we live with purpose like that, we ultimately discover that happiness will follow us.

CONCLUSION

———

*"You may not end up where you thought
you were going, but you will always end
up where you were meant to be."*

—ANONYMOUS

When I started writing this book, I believed wholeheartedly
in the premise that the most worthwhile thing we can do
with our lives is to find our purpose. But I thought it had to
be some big grand thing that I did—like starting a ministry
to impact thousands of people or, ironically, writing a book.
For the longest time, those ideas felt disconnected from my
reality and left me feeling overwhelmed, not knowing where
to start. But researching these stories and reflecting on my
own journey allowed me to see that it is about finding ways
we can bring meaning to everything we do. I realized our
purpose has no size requirement—no expression is too small.
It can be as simple as loving one person in our life or changing our motivation behind the things we do. The little steps

we take add up over time and train our awareness to recognize the more significant opportunities that come along the way—which is exactly what led me to act on the chance to write this book. Purpose will find us if we are willing to simply take the first step and keep following it up with another.

I mentioned in the introduction how my journey to purpose was set in motion after I read *The Purpose Driven Life* by Rick Warren. It sparked a series of events in my life that brought me to find purpose and eventually discover the opportunity to write a book of my own. I now hope that I can do the same for you and ignite your desire to live with purpose. But it shouldn't end with you—that is simply the beginning. It is up to you now to accept this charge to find your own opportunity to influence others so you can leave a legacy and pass on the torch of purpose to the next generation.

The challenge will be staying focused on this quest amid the influence of our culture that constantly tells us finding happiness is what life is all about. We must recognize the bombardment of social media posts and advertisements that seek to make us feel discontent by convincing us we would be happy *if we only had (blank)*. These influences will draw our attention to idolize our level of enjoyment in life above everything else. If left unchecked, it will impact our decisions, from relationships to career choices—as we end up evaluating everything based solely on how happy it makes us feel.

But now we know making happiness our guiding light doesn't lead us where it promises. Instead of bringing us to a place of enduring joyfulness, it leaves us unfulfilled, longing for something more. It forces us to maintain a state of emotion that depends on how we are feeling. We witnessed this in the story of Michael Phelps, who retired at a young age to pursue his happiness full time. Instead of reaching a state of blissful contentment, he found himself in one of the lowest moments of his life. Chasing happiness seems like chasing the wind—we may feel it at times, but it is constantly changing directions.

My experience in high school showed me this firsthand when I based my decisions on the same motivation. I partied and pursued relationships, hoping to find happiness. But once I discovered God created me for a purpose, it caused a complete paradigm shift in me as I realized my life had greater meaning. I stopped trying to fill my life with things that would make me happy and instead turned to see how I could fill the world with my purpose. That decision revealed my passion for helping others discover their unique calling and the meaning behind the life they were meant to impact the world with. It compelled me to write this book to remind people that there is a more worthwhile journey out there, just waiting for them. That our greatest joy will come once we step off the treadmill of happiness and into the pursuit of purpose.

The question I faced after discovering this was: how do I know what my purpose is? How do I go about finding my calling? That is the big question that begins our quest. But the confusion that can come from trying to find the answer can be very discouraging. In order to help answer this, we looked at five stories of people who each possessed a different principle that led them to find their calling. Those principles became the building blocks of purpose that gave us ideas of how to build meaning within our lives:

- **Passion:** Adam Braun showed us that passion is an essential place to look for meaning. We are passionate about things for a reason, and following those passions is a necessary first step.

- **Authenticity:** Brené Brown taught us we need to own our story—all of who we are—by being vulnerable. Being truly authentic will allow us to see the purpose behind the unique ways we were designed.
- **Pain:** Rebekah Gregory taught us that out of our deepest pain in life can emerge the most profound platforms for purpose. Listening to the experiences we have gone through can unlock immense meaning.
- **Love:** Welles Crowther showed us that true love is placing others before ourselves. That type of unconditional love is essential to serving others and expressing our purpose.
- **Opportunities:** Scott Neeson's story reminded us we all have unique opportunities that only we can take hold of—when we recognize them, the path forward becomes clear.

As we look at these stories, each person exemplified a completely different life than the narrative of pursuing happiness our culture points us to. They made decisions that were not based on what made them happy but on what they felt like they were called to do. They poured out of their lives different resources to help others instead of focusing intently on how they could help themselves fill up on whatever they thought would make them happy. The irony is they are indeed happy with their lives, but they didn't get there by chasing it—they got there by pursuing purpose and finding their calling.

If you started this journey with a longing for something more—because of the lack of fulfillment in your life or because you had a deeper desire to do something great but didn't know where to start—I hope you can now see the clear path forward to alleviate your restlessness and find true fulfillment. My prayer is that you would be emboldened and empowered to live with purpose as you look at your life with a fresh new perspective. Let's replace the feeling of emptiness with significance as we stop trying to fill our lives with stuff and start filling the world with our God-given purpose.

As you think through all that we have discussed, I hope you will seek to answer this question: *"What purpose am I meant to express with my life?"* Consider that question both in the context of your normal everyday routines and within each big life decision you face. The answers we find when we look to our building blocks of purpose will help us create a meaningful life. With our focus set on this question, we will grow more aware of the purpose our life holds and keep heading toward significance. This is only the starting point of our new journey. There is no telling where it will take us—but, in the end, it will be well worth it.

ACKNOWLEDGMENTS

———

I would like to honor and thank everyone who contributed to making this book a reality. It would not have been possible without the generosity, support, and encouragement of so many people.

First and foremost, thank you to my Lord and Savior Jesus Christ for pursuing me with your grace that redeemed my life and gave me purpose. For your guidance, which inspired and led me to the opportunity to write this book.

Thank you to my entire family for your generosity, encouragement, and belief in me. Mom, Dad, Jord, Kels—thank you for your unwavering support and unconditional love that helped shape the person I am today and for instilling in me the attitude that I can do whatever I set my mind to. Mammer and Papa, thank you for your remarkably generous spirit and for always seeing the best in me.

To Bill—thank you for agreeing to mentor me when I shook your hand at church and giving me an incredible opportunity to fulfill my calling to serve others as an advisor.

To Andy—thank you for your sage counsel that helped me through my most challenging moments in life to become a better version of myself.

To Rory—thank you for your mentorship that led me out of my crazy college kid ways and into the life of purpose that God had for me.

To Lindsey—thank you for showing me it's possible to do this and introducing me to Eric.

To the team at New Degree Press—thank you for the tools, resources, and talented people that helped make this book a reality. Special thanks to Eric Koester for teaching me how to write a book and share my message with the world. To my editors Jesse Rivas for making me a better writer and Cynthia Tucker for keeping me on track through all my revisions.

To my beta readers: Mom, Bill, Chris—thank you for taking the time to pour detailed feedback over my manuscript.

Finally, I would like to thank everyone who texted, commented, and supported me on this journey. For those who shared *The Pursuit of Purpose* with others to help build momentum. And a special thanks to the following people for participating in my pre-order campaign by buying one or several copies early to make publishing possible. I am sincerely grateful for your generosity.

Abby Limjoco

Amanda Schuring

Anthony Valdivieso

Becky Burright

Billie McShane

Charles Sherburne

Christy Nolte*

Cynthia Tucker

Emily Preis

Eric Koester

Francisco Vargas

Alisa L. Puchmelter*

Annie Boyle*

Ashley Pabst

Bill Stevenson*

Brent Batiste

Christine Mooney

Claire & Sam Gorick

Deborah Caticchio

Enrika Sinkeviciute

Florentina Daju

Gesa Moje

Hannah Ellis
Jamie Wombacher
Jessica Oltmanns
Joe & Leigh Anne Espinosa*
John Good*
Jordan Wedell*
Kara Koster
Katie Cutinello
Kevin Buck
Lance Dobler
Lindsey Kunz
Lisa Roller
Marcie Sarillo
Marianne Arvanites
Matt Stark
Patricia Cutinello*
Robert LoCascio*
Sara Cassidy
Scott & Jennie Lucido*
Steven Schwabe*
Theresa A Walker-Wedell

Harley Griffiths
Jesse Diaz
Joe & Doris Frangiamore*
John & Cheryl Wedell*
John Ribando
K.C. Loftus
Katherine Keenan
Kelsey Wedell
Kim Schuring
Lei Zhou
Linnea & Mike Corsten*
Luke Zdeb
Maria Gandara
Matt Gandolfo
Michael B. Santos
Rebecca Henze
Rory Fulcher*
Sarah Palmer
Simona Render
Taylor Corsten*

*multiple copies ordered

APPENDIX

INTRODUCTION

CDC, Centers for Disease Control and Prevention. "Leading Causes of Death Reports." Accessed May 8, 2021. https://webappa.cdc.gov/sasweb/ncipc/leadcause.html

CDC, Center for Disease Control and Prevention. "Increase in Suicide Mortality in the United States, 1999–2018." National Center for Health Statistics. Accessed on December 8, 2020. https://www.cdc.gov/nchs/products/databriefs/db362.htm

Cigna. "Loneliness and the Workplace." Combating Loneliness. Accessed on December 8, 2020. https://www.cigna.com/static/www-cigna-com/docs/about-us/newsroom/studies-and-reports/combatting-loneliness/cigna-2020-loneliness-infographic.pdf

Drehs, Wayne. "The Evolution of Michael Phelps." ESPN, The Power of Sports. July 31, 2016. Video Documentary, 15:01. https://www.espn.com/video/clip/_/id/17185805

NIMH (National Institute of Mental Health). "Statistics: Suicide."
Mental Health Information. Accessed on December 8, 2020.
https://www.nimh.nih.gov/health/statistics/suicide.shtml

Pew Research Center. "In U.S., Decline of Christianity Continues
at Rapid Pace" Religion & Public Life. Accessed on December 8, 2020. https://www.pewforum.org/2019/10/17/in-u-s-de-
cline-of-christianity-continues-at-rapid-pace/

U.S. National Library of Medicine. "National Trends in the Preva-
lence and Treatment of Depression in Adolescents and Young
Adults." Accessed on December 8, 2020. https://www.ncbi.nlm.
nih.gov/pmc/articles/PMC5127071/

CHAPTER 1

Crouse, Karen. "Seeking Answers, Michael Phelps Finds Himself." New York Times. June 24, 2016. https://www.nytimes.
com/2016/06/26/sports/olympics/michael-phelps-swimming-
rehab.html

Drehs, Wayne. "The Evolution of Michael Phelps." ESPN, The
Power of Sports. July 31, 2016. Video Documentary, 15:01.
https://www.espn.com/video/clip/_/id/17185805

Freedman, Marc. "Prime Time: How Baby Boomers Will Revolu-
tionize Retirement And Transform America." PublicAffairs,
The Perseus Books Group. United States of America, 1999.

Georgetown Law. "A Timeline of the Evolution of Retirement in
the United States." Georgetown University Law Center. 2010.

https://scholarship.law.georgetown.edu/cgi/viewcontent.
cgi?article=1049&context=legal

Kroft, Steve. "60 Minutes." CBS News. June 2005. https://www.
cbsnews.com/news/transcript-tom-brady-part-3/

Meslow, Scott. "Josh Radnor Wants You to Move on From How I
Met Your Mother." GQ. March 13, 2018. https://www.gq.com/
story/josh-radnor-wants-you-to-move-on-from-how-i-met-
your-mother

Moore, Andrew. "Hedonism." The Stanford Encyclopedia of
Philosophy. Winter 2019 Edition. https://plato.stanford.edu/
archives/win2019/entries/hedonism/

Newberry, Paul. "Phelps Says Mental Health is New Passion." AP
News. May 22, 2018. https://apnews.com/article/580834307361
4d6897f6577d43f053d0

PBS. "The Rise of American Consumerism." American Experience.
Accessed May 8, 2021. https://www.pbs.org/wgbh/americanex-
perience/features/tupperware-consumer/

SSA.gov. "Historical Background and Development of Social Security." Social Security Administration. Accessed May 8, 2021.
https://www.ssa.gov/history/briefhistory3.html

Warren, Rick. "The Purpose Driven Life: What on Earth Am I
Here For?" Grand Rapids: Zondervan, 2002.

Welch, Head. "I can't Stop: The Grip of Addiction & Fatherhood." I Am Second. April 19, 2012. https://www.iamsecond.com/film/brian-welch/

Wilbon, Michael. "Why Phelps Isn't Lying: He's Done." ESPN. August 4, 2012. https://www.espn.com/olympics/summer/2012/story/_/id/8234378/2012-olympics-believe-michael-phelps-done

CHAPTER 2

Frankl, Viktor. "Man's Search For Meaning." Beacon Press. Boston, MA. 1949.

Howes, Lewis. "Blake Mycoskie: TOMS Shoes Founder on Changing Business and The World." December 23, 2018. Video, 1:09:51. https://www.youtube.com/watch?v=domK3ylcmQ4

Frankl, Viktor. "Man Alive." Interviewed by Ray Bonisteel. CBC Television, Canada. 1977. https://youtu.be/hX4eaMUiIwo

Warren, Rick. "The Purpose Driven Life: What on Earth Am I Here For?" Grand Rapids: Zondervan, 2002.

CHAPTER 3

Amazima Ministries. "Celebrating 10 Years of Ministry!" Accessed May 8, 2021. https://amazima.org/impact/

Amazima Ministries. "Our Story." Accessed May 8, 2021. https://amazima.org/about-us/our-story/

Begley, Sharon. "Science Finds God." Newsweek, Inc. 1998. https://www.washingtonpost.com/wp-srv/newsweek/science_of_god/scienceofgod.htm

Davis, Katie. "Kisses From Katie: A Story of Relentless Love and Redemption." Howard Books, A Division of Simon & Schuster, Inc. New York, NY. 2011.

Warren, Rick. "The Purpose Driven Life: What on Earth Am I Here For?" Grand Rapids: Zondervan, 2002.

CHAPTER 4

3M. "History Timeline: Post-it® Notes." Accessed May 15, 2021. https://www.post-it.com/3M/en_US/post-it/contact-us/about-us/

Donnelly, Tim. "9 Brilliant Inventions Made by Mistake." Inc. Magazine. August 15, 2012. https://www.inc.com/tom-foster/mike-doehla-strongeru-2020-inc5000.html

CHAPTER 5

Braun, Adam. "How to Change The World & Live Your Purpose." Interview by Marie Forleo. March 18, 2014. https://www.marieforleo.com/2014/03/change-the-world-adam-braun/

Braun, Adam. "Adam Braun: How He Started Pencils of Promise." Good Life Project: Interview by Jonathan Fields. Accessed January 8, 2021. Video, 36:38. https://www.goodlifeproject.com/podcast/adam-braun/

Jeffrey, Scott. "Core Value List: Over 200 Personal Values to Discover What's Most Important to You." CEOsage. Accessed June 22, 2021. https://scottjeffrey.com/core-values-list/

MidAmerica Nazarene University. "America's Dream Job." Accessed May 14, 2021. https://www.mnu.edu/graduate/blogs-ideas/americas-dream-job

Pencils of Promise. "How We Track Our Progress." Accessed May 14, 2021. https://pencilsofpromise.org/results/

U.S. Marine Corps. "Marine Corps Values." Accessed May 14, 2021. https://www.marines.com/life-as-a-marine/standards/values.html

CHAPTER 6

Brown, Brené. "The Power of Vulnerability." Filmed at TEDxHouston June 2010 in Houston, TX. TED Video, 20:02. https://www.ted.com/talks/brene_brown_the_power_of_vulnerability?language=en

Brown, Brené. "Listening to Shame." Filmed at TED Conference. March 2012.

Brown, Brené. "Daring Greatly: How the Courage to be Vulnerable Transforms the Way we Live, Love, Parent, and Lead." New York, NY: Avery, 2015.

Brown, Brené. "The Gifts of Imperfection: Let Go of Who You Think You're Supposed to Be and Embrace Who You Are." Center City, Minnesota: Hazelden Publishing, 2010.

Bruce, Clare. "From Abused to Unashamed: Christine Caine's Story." Hope Media LTD. April 26, 2016. https://hope1032.com.au/stories/life/inspirational-stories/2016/from-abused-to-unashamed-christine-caines-story/

Young, Sarah. "Rising from the Ashes of Abuse: Christine Caine & Jennifer Clinger." Jesus Calling Podcast. Accessed May 15, 2021. https://www.jesuscalling.com/podcast/rising-ashes/

The Enneagram Institute. "Sign up to receive an EnneaThought® for the Day email." Accessed June 21, 2021. https://subscriptions.enneagraminstitute.com/subscribers/create

The Enneagram Institute. "The Nine Enneagram Type Descriptions." Accessed June 21, 2021. https://www.enneagraminstitute.com/type-descriptions

Your Enneagram Coach. "Enneagram Type Assessment." Accessed June 21, 2021. https://assessment.yourenneagramcoach.com/

CHAPTER 7

Bever, Lindsey. "'Dear Dzhokhar Tsarnaev': A survivor's letter to the accused Boston bomber." Washington Post. March 5, 2015. https://www.washingtonpost.com/news/morning-mix/wp/2015/03/05/dear-dzhokhar-tsarnaev-a-boston-marathon-survivors-letter-to-the-man-who-maimed-her/

Enwemeka, Zeninjor. "Boston Marathon Bombing Survivor Writes Letter to 'Coward' Dzhokhar Tsarnaev." WBUR News. March 5, 2015. https://www.wbur.org/news/2015/03/05/boston-marathon-bombing-survivor-letter-to-dzhokhar-tsarnaev

Gregory, Christina PhD. "The Five Stages of Grief: An Examination of the Kubler-Ross Model." PSYCOM. May 4, 2021. https://www.psycom.net/depression.central.grief.html

Gregory, Rebekah. "From Pain to Purpose." Podcast. https://paintopurposepodcast.com/

Gregory, Rebekah. "Inspiring Stories: Rebekah Gregory." Interview by Jim Nicodem. Christ Community Church. November 6, 2017. https://vimeo.com/241550167

Gregory, Rebekah. "Rebekah Gregory, Boston Marathon Bombing Survivor: 'I've Found My Purpose in Life.'" Interview by Peter Alexander. NBC News. March 5, 2015. https://www.nbcnews.com/news/us-news/boston-marathon-bombing-survivor-ive-found-my-purpose-life-n318026

Gregory, Rebekah. "Taking My Life Back: My Story of Faith, Determination, and Surviving the Boston Marathon Bombing." Grand Rapids: Revell, 2017.

James, Susan Donaldson. "Boston Marathon Survivor Rebekah Gregory Asks for Prayers for Preemie Daughter." TODAY. May 10, 2016. https://www.today.com/health/boston-marathon-survivor-rebekah-gregory-asks-prayers-preemie-daughter-t91606

Jones, Ashley. "Ashley's Story." Love Not Lost. Accessed May 15, 2021. https://lovenotlost.org/ashleys-story

Kessler, Julie. "A Mission Close to Our Hearts." Picture This Organized (blog). March 17, 2018. https://www.picturethisorganized.com/love-not-lost/

Lupkin, Sydney and Alana Abramson. "Boston Marathon Bombing Survivor Crosses Finish Line." ABC News. April 20, 2015. https://abcnews.go.com/Health/boston-marathon-bombing-amputee-crosses-finish-line/story?id=30455027

Tull, Matthew PhD. "How Journaling Can Help With PTSD." Very Well Mind. December 14, 2020. https://www.verywellmind.com/how-to-use-journaling-to-cope-with-ptsd-2797594

CHAPTER 8

Burton, Neel M.D. "These Are the 7 Types of Love." Psychology Today. June 25, 2016. https://www.psychologytoday.com/us/blog/hide-and-seek/201606/these-are-the-7-types-love

Chapman, Gary. "The 5 Love Languages: The Secret to Love That Lasts." Chicago: Northfield Publishing, 1992.

Compassion International. "History of Compassion International." Accessed May 18, 2021. https://www.compassion.com/history.htm

Compassion International. "Child Sponsorship FAQ." Accessed May 18, 2021. https://www.compassion.com/sponsor_a_child/sponsorship-faq.htm

Botelho, Greg and Maria Hinojosa. "The Man in the Red Bandana." CNN, America Remembers. September 11, 2002. http://www.cnn.com/SPECIALS/2002/america.remembers/stories/heroes/welles.html

Grey Dog Media, LLC. "Compassion International." Life Beautiful Magazine, Faith. Accessed May 18, 2021. https://lifebeautifulmagazine.com/faith/compassion-international

Kilgannon, Corey. "Saved on 9/11, by the Man in the Red Bandanna." NY Times. September 8, 2017. https://www.nytimes.com/2017/09/08/nyregion/welles-crowther-man-in-red-bandanna-911.html

Greer, Peter and Chris Horst. "A Tale of Two Presbyterian Ministers: Mission Drift at the World's First Child-Sponsorship Organization." Philosophical Fragments. Blog, Patheos. February 24, 2014. https://www.patheos.com/blogs/philosophicalfragments/2014/02/24/a-tale-of-two-presbyterian-ministers-mission-drift-at-the-worlds-first-child-sponsorship-organization/

Rinaldi, Tom. "SC Featured: The Man in the Red Bandana." ESPN, The Power of Sports. September 11, 2019. Video Documentary, 13:53. https://www.youtube.com/watch?v=S77KYbkmjw-c&t=33s

Rinaldi, Tom. "The Man In The Red Bandana." ESPN, Outside the Lines. September 11, 2016. Podcast, 22:34. https://www.espn.com/radio/play/_/id/17519343

The Five Love Languages. "Quizzes: Learn Your Love Language." Accessed June 22, 2021. https://www.5lovelanguages.com/quizzes/

The White House. "Remarks by the President at 9/11 Museum Dedication." Speeches & Remarks Archive. May 15, 2014. https://obamawhitehouse.archives.gov/the-press-office/2014/05/15/remarks-president-911-museum-dedication

Welles Remy Crowther Charitable Trust. "Welles' Story." Accessed May 18, 2021. https://www.crowthertrust.org/welles-story/

CHAPTER 9

Cooke, Camilla. "An Unconventional Success Story: Scott Neeson of CCF." Cambodian Children's Fund, originally posted on Catalyst MDC. January 5, 2017. https://www.cambodian-childrensfund.org/stories-news/unconventional-success-story-scott-neeson-ccf

CCF (Cambodian Children's Fund). "Scott's Story." Accessed May 19, 2021. https://www.cambodianchildrensfund.org/our-mission/scotts-story

Sinek, Simon. "Start with Why: How Great Leaders Inspire Everyone to Take Action." New York: Portfolio, a member of Penguin Group, 2009.

Wilkinson, Bruce. "The Dream Giver: Following Your God-Given Destiny." Colorado Springs: Multnomah Books, 2003.

Wolfe, Alexandra. "Scott Neeson: From Hollywood Executive to Philanthropist." Wall Street Journal. June 12, 2015. https://www.wsj.com/articles/scott-neeson-from-hollywood-executive-to-philanthropist-1434134269

CHAPTER 10

Bannister, Andy. "Old Truths from Oxford: C.S. Lewis and the New Atheists." C.S. Lewis Institute. Summer 2019 issue of Knowing & Doing. https://www.cslewisinstitute.org/Old_Truths_from_Oxford_CS_Lewis_and_the_New_Atheists

Clayson, Amber. "'Unbroken' faith: The Religious journey of Louis Zamperini." Deseret News. December 18, 2014. https://www.deseret.com/2014/12/18/20555033

Hillenbrand, Laura. "Unbroken: A World War II Story of Survival, Resilience, and Redemption." New York: Random House Trade, 2014.

Lewis, C.S. "Mere Christianity." New York: Macmillan, 1960.

Meroney, John. "'World War II Isn't Over' Talking to Unbroken Veteran Louis Zamperini." The Atlantic. November 11, 2014. https://www.theatlantic.com/politics/archive/2014/11/world-war-ii-isnt-over-talking-to-unbroken-veteran-louis-zamperini/382616/

CHAPTER 11

Becker, Clare. "Five Key Takeaways from WSB Alum and Team Rubicon CEO Jake Wood." University of Wisconsin School of Business: School News. February 24, 2021. https://wsb.wisc.edu/news/school-news-blog/2021/02/24/five-key-takeaways-from-wsb-alum-and-team-rubicon-ceo-jake-wood

Britannica Encyclopedia Online. "Newton's Laws of Motion." Accessed May 30, 2021. https://www.britannica.com/science/Newtons-laws-of-motion

ESPN. "Jake Wood, Team Rubicon Receive Pat Tillman award for service." July 18, 2018. Video, 5:08. https://www.youtube.com/watch?v=YDfdUMdvOhQ

NASA. "July 20, 1969: One Giant Leap for Mankind." Accessed June 10, 2021. https://www.nasa.gov/mission_pages/apollo/apollo11.html

Tedx Talks. "Molding military service for global good." November 6, 2013. Video, 17:57. https://www.youtube.com/watch?v=l6Zf-kWhuU8

Wood, Jake. "A new mission for veterans — disaster relief." Filmed December 2011 in San Diego, CA. TED Video, 4:43. https://www.ted.com/talks/jake_wood_a_new_mission_for_veterans_disaster_relief?language=en

Zaremba, Haley. "How Much Fuel It Takes to Get to the Moon." Business Insider. August 9, 2017. https://www.businessinsider.com/how-much-fuel-it-takes-to-get-to-the-moon-2017-8

CHAPTER 12

Rhimes, Shonda. "My Year of Saying Yes to Everything." Filmed February 2016 in Vancouver, BC. TED Video, 18:23. https://www.ted.com/talks/shonda_rhimes_my_year_of_saying_yes_to_everything?language=en#t-8926

ENDNOTES

———

1 Drehs 2016

2 CDC 2021

3 U.S. National Library of Medicine 2020

4 Pew 2020

5 Pew 2020

6 Wilbon 2012

7 Drehs 2016

8 Newberry 2018

9 Kroft 2005

10 Meslow 2018

11 Welch 2012

12 Georgetown 2010

13 Freedman 1999

14 PBS 2021

15 Moore 2019

16 Howes 2018

17 Frankl 1977

18 Amazima 2021

19 Davis 2011

20 Donnelly 2012

21 3M 2021

22 Braun 2014
23 Braun 2021
24 Pencils 2021
25 Braun 2021
26 US 2021
27 Brown 2010
28 Brown 2010
29 Brown 2010
30 Brown 2012
31 Brown 2010
32 Young 2021
33 Bruce 2016
34 Bruce 2016
35 Gregory 2017
36 Bever 2015
37 Lupkin 2015
38 James 2016
39 Jones 2021
40 Kessler 2018
41 Rinaldi 2019
42 Rinaldi 2016
43 Rinaldi 2019
44 White House 2015
45 Grey 2021
46 Compassion 2021
47 Cooke 2017
48 Cambodian 2021
49 Wolfe 2015
50 Wolfe 2015
51 Wolfe 2015
52 CCF 2021
53 Wolfe 2015